""WaWa" is William Coughlan's absorbing autobiography of an American boy's childhood years in West Africa. The years are the mid-1950s, years when so much was being ventured and, usually, only partially resolved, in areas including the independence of African nations from colonial regimes and the creation of new international markets for huge concerns such the oil company young Coughlan's father worked for. A child is not centrally involved in politics or business, but he sees things--—at home, at school, in the villages, out the windows of the family vehicle. A child may also be more likely to live and learn the languages surrounding him, in part because he will have native playmates and also have a conversational relationship with cooks, drivers, and other adults that his parents might not have, even when they seek those conversations. Coughlan is alternative to what I will call, with respect, the theater of West Africa in the time of his life there. He relates to how West Africans perform in enacting family rivalries, in challenging political opponents, and in negotiating more money or time off from American or European employers. And Coughlan is quite clear about how a West African member of his household could choose to perform in such a way that he, Coughlan, could either get in much trouble or blessedly free of blame, whether or not blame was warranted.

"WaWa" is an acronym for "West Africa Wins Always." What you show know by that thought is that there is often a West African view of life that negotiates the absurdities of Western life, as it invented on both sides of the North Atlantic. In the sound of ""WaWa" is something indicating both resolution and lament: as you find often in this narrative, a tale or even a paragraph can end with the words "WaWa." It is the final sound, final punctuation, if you will, to a story.

William Coughlan's enduring remembrance of what "WaWa" expresses tells us that his experience in West Africa brings fresh meaning to that special quip: "I got a good colonial education." With that education, he could see all the world he would experience, even as a boy, in special terms."

—Robert B. Stepto,- author of Blue as the Lake: A Personal
Geography and of a World Elsewhere: Reading
African American Classics in the Age of Obama.
Professor of African American Studies, American Studies
and English, Yale University

WAWA-WEST
AFRICA

A coming of age memoir

WILLIAM COUGHLAN JR.

BALBOA.
PRESS
A DIVISION OF HAY HOUSE

Balboa Press books may be ordered through booksellers or by contacting:

Balboa Press
A Division of Hay House
1663 Liberty Drive
Bloomington, IN 47403
www.balboapress.com
1-(877) 407-4847

Because of the dynamic nature of the Internet, any web addresses or links contained in this book may have changed since publication and may no longer be valid. The views expressed in this work are solely those of the author and do not necessarily reflect the views of the publisher, and the publisher hereby disclaims any responsibility for them.

The author of this book does not dispense medical advice or prescribe the use of any technique as a form of treatment for physical, emotional, or medical problems without the advice of a physician, either directly or indirectly. The intent of the author is only to offer information of a general nature to help you in your quest for emotional and spiritual well-being. In the event you use any of the information in this book for yourself, which is your constitutional right, the author and the publisher assume no responsibility for your actions.

Any people depicted in stock imagery provided by Thinkstock are models, and such images are being used for illustrative purposes only.
Certain stock imagery © Thinkstock.

ISBN: 978-1-4525-3349-0 (sc)
ISBN: 978-1-4525-3351-3 (hc)
ISBN: 978-1-4525-3350-6 (e)

Library of Congress Control Number: 2011904220

Printed in the United States of America

Balboa Press rev. date: 9/8/2011

PREFACE

WaWa stands for West Africa wins again. It is pronounced Wah-Wah. As it falls off your lips, as the blurbs mentioned, it means the end of that particular story. It is like a West African laugh at the contradictions brought to Africa by Americans and Europeans. It is a laugh to off set the colonial view of the world. It is a point of cultural resistance to the colonial point of view. The reader is asked to find humor where he may not have found it before. Though it is repetitive, it is so because it takes a while to build up the many understandings of WaWa, a reader may need to adopt it for himself. WaWa is both personal and general. That is to say, sometimes it is a personal joke, such as the time my brother and I thought the air- conditioning noise was a lion roaring at a distance.

Other times, it might be a statement of wisdom, where a canoe that turns over in the surf where by a fisherman loses his fish. We laugh with him because laughter is the best medicine to apply to this misery. Because sometimes with misery, this is the only thing we can do. Humor is the cultural asset, and it is a valuable one too. Hence, if you tire of WaWa, don't worry, just WaWa.

—William Coughlan

My brother's recollections of life in West Africa are naturally filtered through the lens of childhood in the 1950's, when the Gold Coast was still under the wing of British colonialism. There are passages that reflect on the political conflict that African resistance to the British engendered, as well as the internal conflict between contending political parties. Perhaps his singular contribution is the claim that social and cultural life in West Africa had its own forms of resistance to visitors from other parts of the world and that—, more often than not—, WaWa prevailed. Certainly West Africa is properly known as the white man's grave as some of this narrative suggests. There were many and various diseases that render the region difficult to live in. During our time in West Africa we all contracted malaria, our mother contracted polio, and my father suffered from dysentery and Hepatitis— among other diseases. Some would argue that the strength and persistence of African traditions in that part of the world is a function of the relatively late and ineffective penetration of Christianity and Islam precisely because of the climate and ecology of the region.

One feature of proud African tradition is the cult of the ancestors, which maintains that one's ancestors can be reborn through the birth of one's children. Of course the corollary to this belief is that if one engages in birth control or other forms of family planning, one is intentionally denying the right of re-birth to one's ancestors. As you might imagine, the depth and prevalence of these beliefs has made family planning initiatives in the region somewhat short-lived.

Another feature of African tradition touched upon in this book is Ju-Ju. While *ju-ju* is not unique to West Africa, it may have originated there. Like the cult of the ancestors, it is a little difficult to know just how pervasive it is. One of the ways these two traditions coincide is in the belief that infertility is evil and that an infertile woman is believed to have been cursed through bad *ju-ju* and that she herself must be shunned lest she, in turn, cast an evil eye on some unfortunate soul.

Ju-ju also played an unfortunate role in the particularly cruel and nasty civil wars that have wracked the region in recent years. This was manifest in the prevalence of child soldiers, women combatants, and tribal / ethnic conflict in Liberia and Sierra Leone.

As my brother's recollections show, WaWa also refers to the uniquely African, sense of humor, which can be puzzling to the Western observer. We might wonder why the West African might find it funny that a canoe tipped over in the surf when the results might mean economic hardship for the family involved. For the West African, Humor is, of course, a buffer against bad luck and adversity— and for that, West Africans are blessed indeed.

—Reed Coughlan PhD.

ACKNOWLEDGEMENTS

This book was started in the early 1970s. At this point, I wish to acknowledge the editorial support of my good friend Liza Bingham for her early support of this manuscript, as well as those the efforts of Patricia McGrath (among others) who kept the hope of this book alive. The method I used to write this book was to keep ideas notebooks that contained a working draft of this manuscript. Over the years, the project grew into a full- fledged book. Then in 2009, I began to circulate the manuscript to a number of friends and colleagues for their critical review. In the last two years, I had one additional editor, Brooke Willis. And his typist friend, Brian Stefan-Szittai, also helped to bring these notes to life. I also want to thank Hannah David— my youngest contributor to this project— for her typing, corrections, and computer expertise. The manuscript has been seen by many eyes and friendly reviews. Many of my relatives have been also involved in this process. I especially want to thank Reed Coughlan and Jonathan Coughlan for their contributions. All my friends and relatives' suggestions' have been incorporated into this final product. The lesson here I believe is "patience and perseverance" have their own reward when writing a book.

I wish to thank my parents even though they have passed on for making this whole experience possible. I wish to thank my Aunt Peggy Howe for her interest and support, Sarah Hill my cousin for her interest and support, for my stepmom Annie Coughlan, as well as the many other relatives who were aware of this project.

Finally, I must thank my wife, June B. Coughlan, for her continued patience, support, and critical assessment of this manuscript as well. Without her, this project would have never been finished. In fact, over the last twenty years, she has helped everything about this manuscript including a dramatic rescue at one point of the only existing copy.

WAWA-WEST AFRICA

DECEMBER 15, 1954

Before we moved to West Africa, I remember how impressed I
was with the Native American girl who could eat rocks. She lived
around the bend in the road from our little red house in Balmville,
New York, in 1954. I don't know if she really swallowed the rock,
but whenever she went to school and came back on the school bus,
she would make it a point to pick a few pebbles from the stream
by the side of the road, wash them off, pop them into her mouth,
and go to her house, and leaving me wondering.

It is in that impressionable time that my father came home
and announced to us that were all going to Africa. At that time,
my father worked for Mobil Oil Company (USA). He was in
the process of transferring to Mobil International. Since it was
not unusual for us to move I have become used to it. This was
my family's fourth move in nine years. That we are moving
to Africa was, at first, no more significant than moving to
Baltimore.

I continue to spend my afternoons playing in the woods. There
I use branches to sweep leaves from the ground to make a network
of paths. There are many kinds of paths; first there is the little path

1

for my construction equipments and toys that I move from one construction site to another. I make them by sweeping the leaves aside by hand. But I discover I am not the only one making paths in the woods, where I find trails started by rabbits and dogs, and I enlarge them to make a network of intermediate paths that could be used for shortcuts and fast getaways.

There is also a series of well- trodden paths between the brown fort house, the secret swinging vine, the rock fort, the dirt cave under the roots of the blown-down trees, and the large oak tree we had surrounded with bush and brambles. Finally, there is the really secret path that could be swept only a little; otherwise they will be too easy to see because small animals made them.

I played out in the woods with Bucky Lybolt, my friend who always wore the combat boots I wanted, that my mother refused to buy for me. Bucky is two years older and did not care much for making paths, but he likes to wrestle or light fires with the leaves and smoke cigarettes. My brother Reed is a curly red-head like me, but is a two- year- younger version. He would have liked to join us, but we didn't want him with us. But this would change, as we will see.

JANUARY 1, 1955

It's time for us to leave for the New York hotel, where we can catch a few hours' sleep because we sold the little red house before setting out for the airport. We leave the city before dawn. Driving down the empty streets, we pass row after row of streetlights, all turning together into waves of red, yellow, and green. This is my last image of America before we are swallowed up by the stubby-winged double-decker Stratocruiser.

Aboard the plane with my brothers and parents, I'm seated next to a man from the U.S. State Department. Traveling seems to be a time when adults take me seriously, so I'm talking with him at great length about the relations between the Soviet Union and the U.S. I feel sure that the people of both countries don't hate each other, and surely I say, "The governments will be able to work something out." He is patient and encouraging, but he makes me aware that there is more to the question than I think. It's heavy stuff to be treated seriously at nine years old. We're talking, and as the sun is coming up; I watch the water below become like my grandfather's face: wrinkled close up but smooth at a distance.

JANUARY 2, 1955, THE NIGHT

The plane flies and flies; vibrating, roaring, and flying on. Late the second night, it lumbers into the Azores, where it has to refuel because planes in 1955 needed to, and then it takes off again. After visiting the captain in the cockpit, there isn't much to do, besides going to the observation/cocktail lounge. My second brother, Reed, and I spend hours there, drinking Cokes and flattening our noses against the glass window, straining for a glimpse of Africa. My youngest brother, Coagie, sleeps on, since he is seven years younger. As I return to my seat, I fall into a deep sleep. I dream of a beach where friendly African girls play with me on fallen palm trees.

I awake to find myself still inside the plane, and I begin to understand that this move is going to be quite different from all the others my family has made. I begin to miss my dogs, Café and George. This is the first move where we have had to leave them behind. I feel bad; I didn't say good-bye to them.

I am lulled again to sleep, thinking about our little red house, the woods, and my friend Bucky Lybolt, whom I'll probably never see again. I wake up as the plane's propellers slow, their blurred circles transforming back into stubby single blades. Through the window, I can see the painted sign in the floodlights: *Accra Airport*, and the afterthought in smaller print: *Elevation 800 feet above sea*

3

level. Excitement chases the sleep from my body. Accra Airport at 2:30 in the morning is subdued. We quickly descend from the airplane and head for customs. At first glance, West Africa seems calm and reassuring. The warm night breeze brushes my skin and all is quiet except for the twinkling of the stars and lights.

We walk past sleepy passengers mumbling to each other in what sounds something like English but is difficult to understand. Before my brother Reed and I can investigate (Coagie is still asleep in my mother's arms), we are through the customs area. We find our suitcases on the other side, all marked with chalk and piled in front of a group of Africans and Europeans waiting for our arrival. Introductions are made but excitement blurs the event. The next thing I know, Reed and I are shown to a car. We get into the back seat while two Africans, one broad-shouldered, the other thin, get into the front, and off we go in a procession.

One thing for sure, Africa starts out with the promise of being different. Reed and I are in a separate company car with someone to drive us – —quite a change from the United States. Our colonial experience has begun.

It is pitch black outside, and all we can see is the black tarmac floating up as the car speeds between the cut red dirt ditches on either side of the road ; and the blanket of night has swallowed everything into shapeless but suggestive forms. The few streetlights string alongside do little to illuminate the landscape. The minutes pass, the car slows, and the shape of a large tree stretches over the outline of a hill that appears. We turn into a black wall through a shallow part of the cut red ditch, and the black becomes gray as the road turned into a dust storm behind us. Then it becomes a red dust storm. Bushes and trees take on more shape as a fence of concrete posts and string wire appear.
Another right turn and we have arrived at our new house. My brother and I climb the stairs into a dining room, where a line of

Africans and Europeans introduce themselves. All I can remember afterwards is a series of warm, friendly handshakes. At the end of the line we find a large living room and a larger veranda that stretches around and down a wing of the house. But before we can explore further, Reed and I are shown our room, which has its own separate bathroom, right next to the veranda and are ushered off to bed. Coagie is put in a bedroom next to our parents, down a hallway and past the veranda.

We are lying in our beds in our new house, wide awake. We begin to talk about what little we have seen so far and as we did, it seems to me I can hear a roaring in the distance. I ask Reed if he can hear it. He says it sounds like lions. There is a long silence with that thought, until I suggest we try to get some sleep and explore in the morning. We are awake another hour, tossing and turning.

JANUARY 3, 1955

Soon, it is morning. Reed and I jump out of bed into our T-shirts, blue jeans, and sneakers, and set out of our air-conditioned bedroom into the warm African sunshine.

The first things we notice are the lizards. They are everywhere, and come in two types: the green ones, which are two to two -and -a -half inches long, and the red-hooded ones, about six inches long. Reed and I watch these lizards for a short while before we decide they are reincarnated push-up champions; every few minutes one or the other (or both) pushes itself up and sinks down again. Sometimes, as we later learned, they will even do push-ups on the ceiling; that is fine except when they fall off and land in breakfast bowls or pots of soup. Meanwhile, we find that these lizards can run faster than either one of us. The race leads us down the driveway to the wire-fence and on with our anticipated lion hunt.

At the driveway gates, we are disappointed to hear no sound of lions. We turn back to the compound. There is plenty to see inside the fence. My brother and I begin our investigation. We find a croquet set, two guava trees, some pineapple plants, and loads of flower beds and flowering bushes. Swarms of red ants are marching up and down the trunk of the tree in the middle of the driveway loop.

Looking up at the branches, we can see nests of green leaves, mysteriously held together. Reed and I begin to throw rocks, hoping to knock a nest down and get a closer look. The first nest we hit bursts open and sprays ants all over us. We run away, screaming and yelling into our new bathroom where, behind closed doors, we turn on the shower, remove our T-shirts, and rinse off the ants. In our hurry, we have clogged the drain with ants and are unable to turn off the shower. The water begins to back up. Reed and I close the bathroom door and go for breakfast, trying to forget the whole problem.

At breakfast, we are quieter than usual. Our father, noticing this, wonders aloud if we are feeling all right. I want to say no, because I can see the water creeping towards the dining room. As luck will have it, my father has to leave for work before the water spreads too far and before our mumbled responses raise any suspicion on his part.

As soon as my father leaves, my brother and I race each other to the kitchen, thinking that George, the first steward (i.e., the chief butler) we met the previous evening, will help. When we get to the kitchen we discover that the first steward's real name is not George but Abel.... Abel explains to us that when my parents have made the mistake of calling him George the previous evening, Abel didn't want to seem rude by correcting them. Armed with that knowledge, it seems easier to get Abel (aka George) to help out with the impending flood. Fortunately for us the floor is made of stone and the water has not backed out past the bedroom door.

After Abel helps Reed and me to mop up the bathroom, and parts of the bedroom, we return to the kitchen to meet the new additions to our family: all the Africans working for us. There is Zilbare, the French-trained cook, and his assistant, Joss. Zilbare is married and has three *pickens* (pidgin English for children). The second steward's name is Robert. (He is second in command and helps Abel). Then there is John, our small boy (the third steward helps do things that Abel and Robert have him do). Teresa, our nanny, is also there; her primary duties are to take care of Coagie.

Finally, we go outside to meet the outside help: this includes Isefu, our gardener, Isefu's assistant [Joseph], and Samuel, the driver, as well as the night watchman Fredrick whom we will meet later today. There is also a gardener's assistant (who is George). The household is larger than what our mother is used to. She has always managed single-handedly. Now she has to manage an entire team of people to run the household.

Just then introductions are interrupted by a loud scream coming from the direction of Coagie's bedroom – actually his bathroom. Reed and I chase down the hall into Coagie's bathroom, where we find my mother and Teresa screaming at the sight of an eight-inch millipede in the drain of the shower. Coagie thinks it is a new toy and is about to pick it up, but the screaming interrupts him.

Abel comes running into the bathroom with the extended broom and hits the millipede 10 or 12 times with it. Quickly losing interest, Reed and I wander off to explore the rest of the neighborhood.

Reed and I are still looking for the lions as we go outside again. We notice the lions' roar seems to come from the front of the house. Reed and I race to the front of the house towards the sounds, only to realize that the roar isn't a lion at all, it is our air conditioners! WaWa, as we say, West Africa wins again. Where else would we think this?

There is more to explore behind the house and between the help's quarters, where there is a chicken-wire enclosure. There are some scrawny chickens and what we are told are peahens, which have been living there before they arrive on our table. Peahens, unlike peacocks, have not much going for them except for their ability to make noise. They can screech loud and long, as Reed and I find by prodding them with sticks, until Zilbare the cook says he will do the same to us. We quit in fear, wondering if he will tell our parents.

Reed and I press on, finding fruit trees in the backyard. We find some guava trees and taste the fruit for the first time. Isefu shows us how to tell which are ripe, and how to avoid the unsavory experience of biting into the green ones before we try and spit the bitter flesh out.

Soon after Dad returns from work, we all go for lunch into the big house. There, Zilbare's French training produces a delicious soup (in some cases, made with the lizards that fell from the ceiling), followed by Boeuf Bourguignon, followed by homemade éclairs. It is great. On top of that, Dad gives each of us a two-shilling piece for our allowance. Then Dad and Mom go off with Samuel driving in a great red cloud of laterite dust to see which schools they can send us to, since they felt it is important for us boys to be busy.

Fascinated by my two-shilling piece, I place the coin into a large matchbox. Then I rattle it back and forth over the couch that I am lying on. Somehow, as I do this, the matchbox opens at the exact moment when I yawn— resulting in me swallowing the two-shilling piece. It is lodged just above my breastbone, where I can feel it with my finger. This causes an immediate uproar in the household. Abel and Teresa hold me upside down and pound on my back until I yell at them to stop. Abel calls the schools that my parents have gone to. They come back so fast that their red laterite trail can be seen a mile away.

Though we are driving to the hospital at top speed over the tarmac, it still takes us half an hour to get there. They place me on a hospital bed, trying to spoon- feed me tea with condensed milk, which I periodically throw up.

At dawn, they wheel me into an operating room. They give me a shot and tell me to count backwards from one hundred. I count thirty-five doctors, orderlies, and nurses before I pass out.

When I awaken, the two-shilling piece is strapped to my wrist, with a sign from some kind soul saying, "Please do not swallow again." I go home with Samuel and my mother, thinking about how I should spend my allowance.

While I am in the hospital, Reed spends his time by making friends with a group of African children at the entrance gate of our compound. This is my first opportunity to meet Alassa and Alakaleen. Alassa is my age and Alakaleen is Reed's. Like us, they are brothers 9 years old and 7 years old, so we decide to go off and visit their house in the nearby village. To get there, we have to walk down the dusty road with the triple- wire fence. The fence has concrete pillars every so often and seems to be for separating our compound from the others and for separating our compound from the space by the sides of the road where people catch buses and mammy wagons up to the big tree we have seen our first night, which stretches over the hill. There, underneath the big tree, sits Alassa's attractive female cousin (Tershisa is her name if memory serves me right.) Next to her is a tray filled with newspaper packages of groundnuts and fried plantains. She also has cola nuts split in half and a charcoal blazer for warming pieces of plantain. Opposite this is a path leading to the village of Alassa and Alakaleen. It is also a local bus and mammy wagon stop.

"The bush" means the area of ground and vegetation (either a road, or a path, or other land) not under cultivation; it's a scrubby bush in clumps with long, dead-looking grass between them. Occasionally, there are tall trees, some of which have evil-looking thorns climbing up them. All of the trees have a main trunk that goes up more than ten feet before spreading out into a canopy. To our young eyes, most of the trees look like carrots with bushes on top. But the one on the top of the hill where our red laterite road meets the black tarmac is different. It is different because it spreads out sideways, as though it has grown that way on purpose to provide protection for the Africans and, on occasion, my brothers and me as we wait for the bus.

At the the base of this tree is the bus and mammy wagon (buses and produce trucks owned and operated by local women) stop on the road to Accra. And this is where my best friend Alassa's cousin's groundnut and hot plantain sales space is located. Fortunately, the red ants do not like this kind of tree. Its trunk and exposed roots have been worn smooth by the many people it provides shade for.

Opposite this is a path leading to the village of Alassa and Alakaleen; across the street is the path to Alassa's village. But it is not in plain view. There is a well-trodden path through a dense collection of younger trees. The path turns and twists so that after 20 twenty feet we cannot see the road, only the top of the shady tree. Then, after fifty or sixty more feet, the open spaces of the mud brick homes appear.

When Alassa, Alakaleen, Reed, and I reach the village, there are a number of small children, some of whom are being held on older children's hips. When they see Reed and me, the younger ones begin to cry. I ask Alassa what the problem is.

"Oh," he says, "their parents told them if they are not good, the white man will come and take them away."

Later on, once they get used to us, they stop crying—but watch us carefully. Alassa and Alakaleen act as though the younger children are foolish and the two of them have known us forever.

Their house is made of red mud bricks and has a thatched roof. Alassa's father is a minor chief in the village, and his people are Hausa. He speaks no English, so Alassa teaches us in Hausa, his tribal language, to say, *"Laufia lo,"* meaning "Greetings." My brother and I quickly pick up this new way of greeting. One pidgin expression my father has trouble with is "WaWa," which literally means, "West Africa wins again," but in deference to his confusion, we often say redundantly: "WaWa West Africa." The meaning of the phrase is humorously demonstrated over and over throughout my time here and elsewhere as well. But some people never seem to catch on.

It is pidgin English that we learn quickly; because most West Africans speak some pidgin English, and our parents ask us to translate for them, particularly when the Hausa traders come by in the evening to sell their crafts to whoever is on the veranda.

Ju-ju is a complex word that Reed, Coagie, and I learn when speaking pidgin and living in West Africa. On the one hand, *Ju-ju* is everything explainable that is happening to you, or between you and other people. It can be regular magic or the most powerful magic. *Ju-ju* can be good or bad. Bad *Ju-ju* can be conjured up by real enemies, unknown enemies, or even by relatives. The best defense against *Ju-ju* is to have strong *Ju-ju* yourself. Sometimes it is best not to mention this about yourself, but let others say that you have strong *Ju-ju* when you did something well. The meaning of *Ju-ju* depends on who is using it: When an adult African uses the words "bad *ju-ju*" to an adult European or American, it means anything can happen, from a WaWa to something dreadful, to nothing. The point is, an African who says, "dat be bad *ju-ju*," that means he isn't going to do the matter at hand. WaWa. Most educated Africans, Americans, or Europeans say that they did do not believe in *ju-ju*. Of course, they too are always talking about who did what to whom, and when and why. But Reed, Coagie, and I do not care. We are only interested in that we need *Ju-ju* too. Today, as we are grown up, we say, "The best plans of mice and men need *Ju-ju* proper number one."

FEBRUARY 5, 1955

It is Alassa's father who taught me something about possessions that I never forgot. Actually, it is Alassa who told me something about his father, which I asked about after we have been friends long enough. I notice that he always took a path in the bush that minimized contact with my clothing, when there were more direct routes to take.

He tells me his father only has two shirts, two smocks (a good one and an ordinary one), and a pair of khaki shorts. He wears the shorts to farm in, with another undershirt in case it is raining and chilly. It surprises me that he has only these few articles of clothing, even though he is the chief of Tesano Village.

I like Alassa's father. He seems a bit more reserved than other adult Africans in the village. Of course, that seems to be because he is chief. If there are problems, they have to resolve them in the Plava House, (a house where tribal problems are discussed) over which he presides. But I am stunned about the clothing, so I ask my dad to explain it to me.

Since I know Dad has said that we have no money (or at least never enough), I want to understand how that can be when Dad has twenty or thirty or more shirts. I know it is normal that

Europeans hire people to work for them in their homes, because that is the way it is. I thought the reason for this is perhaps to give people jobs. Even so, something seems upside down about all this. Dad explains to me that we do not make or have as much money as some "other" people. That explanation does not sit well with me. Besides a television, I cannot think of anything we need. That upside-down feeling has remained with me to this day. WaWa.

Reed and I are quick to admire the slingshots that Alassa and Alakaleen have. So, after practicing with theirs, we commission two of our own, for two shillings apiece. The key to the whole matter is to cut down a good, V-shaped stick, and use it to craft the red rubber inner tube of bicycles (since they stretch better than black rubber) and of course, a nice leather sling to hold the stone. The slingshot is hand-cut from a large piece of brown leather, chewed on to make it soft. Reed and I shoot at birds, lizards, and ants' nests in the trees in front of the house. I even go halfway through my marble collection before I shoot a sparrow through one of our house windows. After that, there are no more slingshots for two weeks.

But for Alassa and Alakaleen, it is a more serious matter. They are responsible for feeding their cats. I get my first taste of what that means when Alassa takes me off of one of the main paths to show me a large pit in the ground. He drops a stone in and some bats fly out. The next time we return with a small-holed net, and beat on the ground around the pit with sticks that we have cut down with machetes. The bats fly into the net, where Alassa grabs them and cuts their throats for his cats. Certainly this is far different from my experience of opening up a tin of cat food.

One afternoon, I see Zilbare, Isefu, and the other help rushing back and forth on the compound between the house and where they live in the help's quarters. I call to Reed and we go running outside. There, running between the Africans is a small diker

13

deer, bleating away. Soon the Africans have it surrounded. Zilbare holds its neck down and cuts it with a sharp knife and the diker begins to twitch. Then Zilbare disembowels it, and begins to cut it up into pieces, and then he puts the pieces in a large pot, some of which he puts right away into his wife's groundnut curry. Reed and I are a bit amazed to see how fast this all occurs and how the diker does look a bit like a small version of Bambi. Reed and I skip that particular curry—, and we don't ask what is in the curry the next time one is boiling outside of Zilbare's quarters either.

FEBRUARY 10, 1955

Soon under Coagie's leadership, all the three of us are eating again, with Zilbare, in his quarters. Stews made from *fou fou, gari*, groundnut, and palm oil stews are the staple, (fou fou looks like mash potatoes that are glazed over, gari looks like grains of large white rice and the stews mentioned look orange and oily) sometimes with a bit of fish or meat. Sometimes as a treat, Zilbare makes *fou fou* for our dinner in the big house when our parents are going out for the evening. But Coagie's leadership will give him away. He will eat so much hot pepper stew that his lips will swell up and there will be an orange ring around them.

"Did you eat at Zilbare's and spoil your dinner?" my parents will ask.

"Oh, no, not me!" he will say, and everyone will laugh.

WaWa.

Zilbare has an assistant, Joss, whom he is training in French, and now in West African colonial cooking. I decide that I can learn how to make the croissants that Zilbare makes so nicely; in return, I will teach him something that I have been taught in school that I think will be enlightening to him about the nature of the universe. I think I know quite a lot and am anxious to proceed with what I think is a fair trade. So, unlike his assistant, I will be an equal, or if I pick the right thing, maybe a superior one to Zilbare's cooking.

Zilbare and Joss are patient and careful to show me how to go through the steps to make croissants. It is a sweet mess of finger-tasty, licky, sticky items that go from stage to stage and that requires both art and science to complete successfully and do just the right thing. At the end, I am not too confident I can get the whole process to work out as easily as Zilbare and Joss do. I figure my idea will make their response a superior one to what I show them.

I go out in the afternoon sun and say, "I will now show you the way the solar system is and how it works." Then I get a stick and draw the configuration of the planets around the sun and put Xs where the planets are symbolically placed, and a large X where the sun is. Then I explain which planets are where, and which one is ours, and how all the planets go around the sun.

Zilbare looks kindly at me and asks, "Can you prove this?"

I take the stick once more and begin to repeat what I have done before. Halfway through, it occurs to me I have no idea how to prove it. I fall silent and become embarrassed. My education leaves me unable to do more than repeat what I have learned. I can say the sun sinks in the west and rises in the east. As for the rest, I am working on repetition.

Zilbare laughs gently. "You do go learn dis *Ju-ju* when you get to be big man."

I am ashamed. I have not thought to respect that he knew the difference between reciting a recipe and knowing some proof, or having some experience. WaWa.

MARCH 7, 1955

In our first home in Tesano, a neighborhood in Accra, my parents sometimes take us to church. The church leaves its doors open due to the heat, but this allows Reed to pick up some red peppers from a red pepper plant growing just outside the church doors on the way in. Reed has been warned by Teresa to never ever, under any circumstances, let red pepper get into his eyes, because he will go blind. Yet he picks a couple and then inadvertently rubs his eyes. Well, he thinks he has done it now. Here he is at church, and God is going to wreak havoc, as he has disobeyed his parents (or *"rents,'* as we used to call them) in church and he has disobeyed Teresa as well. So he gives voice to his terror and begins to scream his head off. It causes my parents some embarrassment, and it takes them some time to calm Reed down enough to find out what has happened. WaWa red pepper = big *ju-ju.*

APRIL 15, 1955

The "Candlestick Affair"—as it came to be known— nearly unglues our relationships with the help, not to mention the "rents". Mom comes home from shopping one day and notices that her favorite candlesticks are bent and twisted. In a commanding voice, almost a scream, she orders Abel, the first steward, Robert, the second steward, and John, the small boy, into the dining room.

"Who did this?" she yells. "Just who did this?"

Abel steps forward. "It is the two oldest boys," he says. "Dey did."

Mother yells for us to come out of the bedroom where we are playing. "Did you do this?" she screams. "Did you ruin my favorite candlesticks?"

"No, Mom," we sing in unison, but we know it is too late to argue. She has made up her mind. Besides, she has heard us protest before when we have done something wrong. It is going to be spanking first, questions later, no matter what. Reed and I know we will have to right this wrong, but we will have to wait until later. Moreover, we understand clearly that this is another way things are in Africa if the help wanted it to be. Teresa can do this with Coagie when the 'rents are out. Everyone except Zilbare the cook, Isefu the gardener, and the night watchman can report us to our parents.

After Reed and I are over the immediate discomfort of the spankings and being grounded after school, Reed talks with me about talking to Mom. We know we have not done the dastardly deed, but we need to have good reasons to prove our innocence. So, we sneak inside the dining room to look at the evidence. Sure enough, the bases are all twisted and turned. In addition, the candlesticks are shiny, as though they have just been polished. Now we know that one of the stewards or the small boy has done this, but what else?

Then Reed holds up one of his hands to my face.

"So what?" I say.

"Our hands aren't strong enough to do this," he says. "It doesn't matter which one of them did it, just show Mom our hands and the candlesticks."

"But what if she gets angry again?" I ask. Then I think to myself, *if we get blamed by everybody for everything, that will be terrible.*

I tell Reed, "Okay. You come with me, and together we'll go to Mom and show her." So we tell Mom, and she makes us go to the living room and tells us to put our hands next to the candlesticks. Mom says nothing to us.

Later, John tells me Abel says it was an accident, and that he had said we boys did it because he is afraid of Madame. Of course, what none of them told us is that if we children did something wrong, all the staff would not to hesitate to tell the 'rents anyway. WaWa.

MAY 15, 1955

If Mom and Dad have known how potentially exciting the movies can get, I'm not sure they would have let us go as frequently. Anyway, we tell them in bits and pieces so they get used to it. Action movies are the only kind Reed, Coagie, Teresa, and I go to. We often sit upstairs in the balcony with the fixed seats. Below are the folding chairs on a wooden floor with a string of lights from the balcony on both sides.

American cowboy movies are the popular fare. These are sure to feature some of our favorite elements: a good guy (or a bunch of them), a gang of bad guys, cows willing in the extreme to run off cliffs, horses that never tire, six- guns that never need reloading, some good weather, and usually a heroine to be rescued—-although Reed, Coagie, and I are not that interested in *that* aspect of it. It really does not matter whether we can anticipate the ending or not. Reed and I are there for the theatre, even though Coagie gets a bit scared. The lights will dim, but not so much that we cannot see figures in the rows downstairs.

The movie and its music will start off and we might have thought that we were in any movie theater anywhere. We can hear a pin drop over the sound of the score. Soon every time the good guy does anything good, we will hear, floating up to the balcony, "Dis be good t'ing" as people, acknowledge the victory of good over evil. If matters happen to be going the other way, we will hear, "You dey be sorry soon." floating up to the balcony. However, when it came to the inevitable battles between groups of good guys and bad guys, the crowd will begin to shut out, *"on ya,"* meaning sort of "give it to them." The audience, especially in the cheapest rows up front, will stand up and wave their fists. As the battle progresses in the movie, so the *"on ya"* quickly become *"on ya somi, on ya toto, on ya gormi."* Now it is personal; groups in the rows begin to take sides and act out mock battles. You never know how far it will go — that depends on the luck of the evening and if the movie has incited the audience sufficiently. The movie operators are skillful in shutting the movie off and bringing up the lights if matters seem too far -gone; that stops the commotion, and the audience settles back down quickly.

I don't know exactly what *"on ya somi, on ya toto, on ya gormi"* translates or means; I only know that after enough things have been said about you, your family, your relatives, and your friends, acting out is called for. Reed, Coagie, and I love it. It is real theatre. It is West African theatre. WaWa.

MAY 20, 1955

Uncle John Shoe Smith is a British fellow who works for the same company as my father. We call him "Uncle John Shoe" because I see him often wearing African clackers, or shoes they are called clackers because they make that noise when we wear them. Uncle John has been in the Queen's Cold Stream Guard and is quite proper, but his laughter is contagious, and Reed and I often hear him on the veranda after we are supposed to be asleep.

On the weekends, either we have a planned curry or go on a picnic to the beach with Uncle John. Zilbare slaughters a fresh chicken or gets some beef from the market and begins to make the curry the night before. The next day, he will cut the meat up and add the various *accouterments* to go on the rice and curry. The guests will arrive and drink pink gins while sitting on wicker chairs on the veranda. They will drink until one of them drops the drink past the holder and it breaks. This is the sign that lunch is to be served. Of course, Reed and I prefer the simple process of going on a picnic with Uncle John. For the most part, the Gold Coast (now called Ghana) beaches have too much undertow to safely go swimming. Reed and I chase the waves up and down the beach and only get our feet wet.

19

There is an exception in pidgin English about the undertow and that is Takoradi (Before Tema Harbor was built), which is the name of the only safe port where ships can enter and there is no surf. When we wanted to say something that is extremely good, out of sight, out of mind, or whatever, we say; "Fine, fine, pass Takoradi" or "Fine, fine, pass Takoradi self" as the ultimate (this is fine, fine because the goods are imported from outside the country and are supposed to be expensive.) Thus Labadi Beach, where we can swim, is "fine, fine pass Takoradi" and Uncle John is "fine, fine, pass Takoradi self; in hindsight it maybe said now Fine, fine pass Tema Harbor.

JUNE 10,19, 1955

I did not have any American kites with me when we arrived in Accra. I see that the African boys have kites at Labadi Beach. We go to the beach every afternoon after missionary school. Actually, the reason Reed and I get to go to the beach so often is that Mom has arranged for us to join the Boy Scouts in Accra, but even though we get uniforms and the basic equipment, we are not allowed to join because we refuse to sing "God Save the Queen.," We are Americans and will only join if we can do the Pledge of Allegiance to the Flag of the United States. Mom offers to have us stand silently, but the scout leader is adamant about this. The scouts, he informs us, are a British invention, and Gold Coast is under British rule. Mom, who ordinarily doesn't back down, since she likes the British, thinks it is easier to just go to the beach each afternoon. Reed and I think that is a better solution too, since the beach is more fun anyway.

I commissioned an African-made kite, and instead of flying at the beach, I take it home and fly it there. Unfortunately, the wind at home is quite similar to the wind at the beach, so the kite will only fly so high and no higher. I test my skills at flying it further and further away from the house, but then the weight of the string can cause the kite to be unable to stay above the bush, and then it will crash. WaWa. I take to flying the kite at a maximum height and distance from the house and simply tie the kite up to the veranda rail. Alassa tells me that some people in the village think I am making ju-ju, since the kite crosses one of the bicycle paths in the bush to another village.

I told him, *"Dis t'ing no be true matter; dis people are foolish for dat side, and I no dey do ju-ju."*

He told me, *"I dey tell them, dey have too much foolish fear and you no be fla-fla boy."* *Fla-fla* is a Ga tribal derogatory curse word used whenever somebody did something wrong. Although Alassa is a Hausa, he still uses the term when it suits him.

Reed and I go to the Hausa village many times. On one visit, we see a man whose legs have swelled so much that he can barely walk. He looks like an elephant with his swollen, stumpy legs. Dad tells us it is similar to a disease that they called Elephantiasis. I tried not to laugh, because it seems so real and so sad all at once that I do not know what to do. After a while, the man also gets malaria and sores developed on his legs. The flies are everywhere in the village, but they find this man a delight. He sits in the sun outside his hut, barely able to move.

I ask Alassa, "What he de do now, dis man?"

Alassa says, "He no dey have money for hospital, he no dey have chicken for *Ju-ju* man. Plenty people say he no dey have powerful *Ju-ju* to stop the *Ju-ju* that others, even his relatives, self-de bring upon him. His relatives want him to die now because otherwise with the Hausa holiday coming, and they have to give five goats for his funeral."

Well, the man soon obliges them all. He up's and dies before the Hausa holiday and the village holds a funeral. This is the first funeral Reed and I ever attend, so we have no idea what to do. Hausa people do not exclude children from adult events, so we can be a part of the ceremony, as long as we did not ask a lot of questions. "Elephant Man," as Reed and I now referred to him, is in a sealed box to one side of the Plava House, (the house where village disputes are resolved by the chief and the elders). The mourners play Talking drums, (light, squeezable drums that have two ends, with strings in between and can be manipulated by squeezing our arms so the sound varies as hard as they are hit. The talking drums start up first, as they are lighter than the regular drums, which are so heavy that they have to stand on their own bases.

A group of the man's female relatives begin to wail and cry. It is not music, but it is not singing, either. Apparently, they knew how to do this from experience. It is like the sound I have heard Arab women on the radio make— piercing and scary. The wailing then turns into crying, and the deeper drums began to beat as the men begin to dance in a circle around the Plava House. Periodically, the men shout out, as if to scare something away something.

"To scare away the evil *ju-ju,* for the man," Alassa whispers in my ear. This goes on for some time, about two to three hours in the blazing sun. The chief, Alassa's father, stands up, and there is silence. He claps his hands twice, and the women bring two goats into the space between the box with the body and the Plava House. The goats have their throats cut, and while the blood is staining the ground, the women begin to wail again. A group of men picks up the coffin with notched wood logs and take it to the fields, with the women following. Alassa, Reed, Alakaleen, and I stay where we are. Alassa says, *"Dis man, he dey have money from his wife's side, but he dey no have Ju-ju to get them to do anything for him. Bad family ju-ju."*

JULY 15, 1955

Winnaba Beach is quite a different kind of beach. It is located at least an hour's drive from Accra, and an hour and a half from Tesano. A number of companies and embassies keep a sort of 1950s version of time-sharing condo arrangements with the two or three beach houses there.

The beach actually has no sand on its waterfront, but is made up of large rocks beaten by heavy surf at high tide. However, what makes swimming possible is a huge concrete pool that sticks out into the surf away from the rocks. At high tide or during storms, the ocean cleans out the concrete pool; otherwise the pool will have only one corner where the surf will splash into. The rest is a salty water haven with the tropical sun flashing off the waters and the shadows of the coconut trees that lined up where the rocks stopped.

Reed and I have no problem with the beach, because we heed the advice of our African friends, who tell us not to enter any small *Ju-ju* house as it is bad for us and bad things can happen to us. Coagie does not listen carefully, so when he sees the small *Ju-ju* house on the beach, he keeps trying to go in and play. My parents do not appreciate his continual efforts.

Reed and I have no trouble with the *Ju-ju* hut, it is true; on the other hand, Winnaba Beach has something else to tell me. Reed leaves me watching the surf on the rocks as he follows up a village path from the beach, away from Accra further up the coast. I go to just look at the tidal pools, and see if I can find any nice- looking coconuts to take home, even though I have only been able to see them up in the trees to that point.

Meanwhile, Reed finds a village, but he did does not enter it. He circles to the left of it. Seeing a bunch of chickens hanging around the village and not much else, he begins to amuse himself by throwing stones at the chickens. Suddenly, a large, warm hand grabs him and drags him into the Plava House.

WILLIAM COUGHLAN JR.

"What kind of fla-fla boy be dis?" the man yells. *"I think maybe I dey go and make your Madame and Master buy all these chickens and I dey tell them you kill two or three more."*

Reed knows this man is serious, and by the time this man tells the 'rents, he elaborates the stoning story, including four or five chickens more, just to make sure he gets a nice "dash" —African for *gift*— to ease the problem. Reed thinks, *"No more slingshots, no more plantains, Billy won't loan me any more money for chocolates, and I'll be grounded for the rest of the beach vacation. Whew! All this for a few pebbles at some scrawny chickens?"*

As the man's voice draws others down the village path, it also draws others from another path— including the path that leads from where the cars are parked on Labadi Beach. Reed sees Samuel, our driver, striding down the path.

"What dey you want with this small boy?" yells Samuel. *"This small picken; what he dey do so you yell at him?"*

Now everybody in the village is in the Plava House. Samuel motions for Reed to sit down and be quiet. The man, who it turns out is the head of the village, begins to tell his story. And sure enough, four or five chickens are supposed to be dead, victims of a vicious attack by my brother.

Then Samuel gets up to speak. *"Dis small boy, he feel sorry for your chickens. He want to see if they be as hungry as they look. He throw small stones to see because if so, he come back to give them food. You look at dis ting,"* Samuel says, and he tosses a pebble near the scrawny chickens and they run over immediately to see what it is. *"So what be dis story of the chickens that be dead? It's only that you dey no feed your chickens at all! This picken worry more about your chickens than you do."*

At this point, applause broke out because, as Samuel knows (and as everybody else knew as well), the headman is a tightwad. "This small boy will get some food for your chickens and then this

24

be *yacatti* (finished)," Samuel announces. Again, there is applause for Samuel's solution, since nobody wanted the head man to have more chickens than he already did, given that he didn't share them with anybody else anyway. Samuel walks Reed back to the beach house to get some bread to feed the chickens. *"If you dey want to be proper picken, you go have proper respect. I know they tell your father because he be ashamed and your father be good man. He be number one man."* Reed told me the story later, and I asked Samuel the rest because I wonder why the headman would give in without trouble. Reed is lucky, but Samuel knew WaWa— and how to use it.

APRIL 30, 1955

When the rainy season arrives in Accra, I get this great idea about building dams underneath the red, sticky ant- nest tree in the driveway. Back in the little red house in Baimville, New York, my great-aunt had sent me a large toy construction set. Initially, she worried that I am a bit too old for the set, but I am into construction (and deconstruction). And, once I have them, I quickly learn and get the idea of how well a steam shovel works by, shoveling sand from our sand pile into dams and buildings. I also learn how well it will work even in the stream by our old house, where I made pools for captured crayfish. Captured crayfish that make crunchy snacks during this are hard work, especially when you light a small fire next to the stream when the 'rents are out.

The deconstruction part is when I smash the windows of our little red tool shed and hammer plywood in their place. Then it is totally dark inside and we can do two things. First, we can imagine all sorts of enemies surrounding us and beat off their attacks with garden tools from all sides. The shack did grow a bit wobbly from all this, but I get ideas about garden tools. Second, there is a wild honeybee nest in the shack, so I think they cannot see me as well in the dark when I get hungry and rob their honeycomb. Still, my parents know what I have done: because the bees in the comb sting the inside of my mouth, and my face swells up, no matter what I say to the contrary.

But the construction toys never made the trip from Balmville to Accra. They got lost on the way. I am left with my deconstruction knowledge of garden tools. The red, sticky ants in Accra have already won the first battle shortly after our arrival. The rainy season in Accra is unusually dry that year, but when it rains, it rains like a dump truck pouring water from the sky. The rain hits the driveway hard and runs off just as quickly as an empty dump truck can, only there isn't another load for quite a while. I take the house and the garden tools and built a number of dams. But each dam is washed away as I experiment with their shapes.

Finally, I make a dam in a U shape that can retain the water and hold it for a while. The water is always red brown and full of laterite dust, yet it will serve my purpose. I repair my dams by using the hose, and the shovel to make mud. Then I wait for another rainstorm. Finally, the rain drops from the sky. I run out before it can finish, my slingshot in hand. This time, I stand some distance away from the ant-infested tree, taking careful aim. I shoot three or four nests of ants down, trying to hit them where they connect with the tree so the nests cannot split apart. With the shovel, I place them in the reservoirs of muddy water. They sail around like six- to eight-inch triangular green ships. The red, sticky ants are stuck; They have to wait until the water dries before they go back up the tree to build new sticky nests, or until their "nests, now ships", are blown close enough to reach land. After a rainstorm, the wind blows in gusts, changing directions. So some of the nests or, rather ships sail in circles. It is an excellent project. WaWa.

SEPTEMBER 1, 1955

Mean while, our parents have enrolled us in a missionary school. Actually, it is more of a private zoo than a missionary school. They have monkeys and parrots, parakeets, canaries, and a host of other birds. It is quite different from the atomic bomb test site we have in the States; there are always quite a number of birds singing and monkeys screaming. Unlike my American schools, we can proceed at our own pace. Somehow I get the impression that when I finish their math books, I will know all there is to know about math and I can quit the topic. It will take another school to dispel that notion.

Then one day, my father brings Linda home. Linda is a Moshie Greyhound, unique to West Africa. Linda can run like the wind; that is, when she is not so obviously pregnant. Reed and I love her and take her everywhere with us, that is at least, when she *consents* to come—even to school, though the monkeys will scream at her quite a bit. But then one day, Linda disappears. Reed and I look everywhere. But she comes back the next day to show us her six brown, shorthaired puppies. In typical African fashion, she had gone into the bush to have her puppies, and when she was ready, she came to show us her new family. Linda definitely loves Reed and me, but she has other friends as well. She has a basket in the garage in which she sleeps with her puppies near the night watchman. The night watchman Richard is also her friend. One night, a spider comes down from the roof and bites Linda. The night watchman sees this happen. With a machete, he cuts a square chunk out of Linda's thigh with the help of Abel and Zilbare. The bleeding causes the poison to run out of the dog. Reed and I thanked Zilbare, Abel, and Richard the night watchman, but he says, "Your father, he be a good man. We know you children be good, too, so this be the right thing to do." WaWa, African people.

Of course, part of it has to do with the fact the night watchman is my friend, too. One day, the night watchman approaches Dad and says, "I dey go come now." Dad says, "Fine."

When he does not return for two evenings, Dad sends me back to the help's quarters to find out what has happened. I find out that "I dey go come now" means "I am leaving now; I ask your permission because (I may not be back for a few days)." African time is not the same as my father's sense of time. Dad thought he would be back in a few hours, or at most the next evening.

When the night watchman does return, I go to him and say, "My father, he say he no dey know this thing 'I dey go come now.' If you want to go for another side [(to another place)] you please dey tell him the whole thing so he dey know." The night watchman thinks about this and then says that my father make proper *"plava"* (talk) and that, "I be number one small boy to find out dis ting," since the night watchman realizes my father does not understand his meaning.

Shortly after that, my mother acquires two Siamese cats from a friend. Both my parents have a soft spot for animals. Mother always thought that the reason Zilbare gave the peahens and chicks a little wine before dispatching them is so they won't feel the pain. But Zilbare told us, "That make tender bird." But when it came to Zilbare, it is a bit of a different story. Every morning, Zilbare serves my father "cold poached egg on plate. " My father sends it back, explaining that there should be toast at least. Zilbare maintains he is a French-trained chef, and as such, he does not make bread. Madame will have to buy it. Then my father just gets some papaya from Zilbare. My father swears to fire Zilbare. But later Zilbare fixes a fabulous lunch for all of us with homemade French cream puffs for dessert, and the argument is over for the day and Zilbare is rehired.

OCTOBER 1, 1955

Samuel drives our mother to the main European store in downtown Accra. Kingsway is just like an American supermarket, only it has a lot of British imported goods. It features loads of chocolates and imported cookies; the British sweet tooth is more varied than even the most expensive American versions. There are far too many to try, though Mom thinks one pound is equal to one dollar (when actually £1 = $2.80), so we get to buy quite a variety. After that, we have to use our allowances. The two shillings that Dad gave us only buy a piece or two of imported candy. Hence, I stick to slingshots, groundnuts, and fresh plantains. Reed ends up borrowing from me because he and Alakaleen are addicted to chocolates.

There is something I always tried to change in Mom's purchases, and that is marmalade. I hate marmalade, particularly orange. I cannot understand how a person would want to ruin perfectly good jam with a bitter orange peel. Mom thinks it is quite the thing to do and always buys it. I have to convince her, Zilbare, and Dad that it is OK to have another kind of jam at breakfast besides marmalade. What a rigmarole! You would have thought that I am asking for blood from a vampire. After a persistent campaign, I get strawberry jam. To think that I have to remember to wear clean clothes, wash my face, brush my teeth, and take baths, and prevent my clothes from getting dirty for a little jam. WaWa, adults are demanding.

There is something else I used to explore while Mom is in Kingsway — the Lebanese shops. They stretch up and down the streets alongside Kingsway. The Lebanese sell anything that Kingsway did or did not, except frozen foods. They sell cloth, jewelry, pots and pans, and anything my house may or may not need. They are a friendly people, so I go and visit with them. I tell them my father doesn't have an oil well just because he works for an oil company. They ask me when they see me, because I am so serious looking, and I explain the difference between wholesale and retail before I figure out that they are only joking.

OCTOBER 30, 1955

Mrs. Kamhaveijam lives down the road from us at Tesano Number One. She and her husband, Kim, are from Egypt, and he works for Dad. Mom and Mrs. Kamhaveijam are good friends. They talk about all sorts of things, including flying saucers, a topic I have overheard my mother talk about in Baimville at her luncheons with close friends. Dad calls Mrs. Kamhaveijam his "European mother-in-law" because she always makes him eat too much when we have dinner at her house. Mrs. Kamhaveijam is a well-known mystic. She reads palms and tarot cards, and provides advice to all who seek it — Europeans and Africans alike. Everyone but me, that is. Every time I ask her, she looks at my hand carefully and then says, "I'm sorry, but your life is just too complicated for me to say right now. Come back another time...and perhaps then." Even though I go back several times; she said says the same thing. I think she is just trying to pique my curiosity. So then I ask my father and then my mother about her. Dad laughs and says Mother had told him that Mrs. Kamhaveijam thinks he is evil because she wanted her husband to be better treated by Dad and pay him more. And Mom told me how Mrs. Kamhaveijam gave Dad a small orange tree that Mrs. Kamhaveijam says will never have oranges. Mom went out and found some small plastic oranges and wired them onto the tree, and Mrs. Kamhaveijam believed that they are real. I remain puzzled and don't understand one iota about what Mom and Dad have said about Mrs. Kamhaveijam, or why she does not read my palms. WaWa, adults are strange.

When we arrive in West Africa, my father has to face *Ju-Ju* and WaWa almost immediately, which many years later I hear as the "soap story." Dad's company embarked on a project to convert from package sales to bulk. Previously, gasoline and kerosene were filled in fifty-five-gallon drums, loaded onto trucks, and distributed to distribution points; hand pumps are fitted to the drums, and direct sales are then made to customers. Kerosene is also sold through sale points and made into two-gallon tins that have the brand logo, and are often re-used for carrying water or palm oil, usually on women's heads, as I recall. The new system is to truck bulk gasoline to service stations, and to service kerosene to sale points in the markets where they installed tanks. In other words, they have to take gasoline sales from drums to the regular pumps, like we have in the United States, and kerosene to bulk sales too.

In order to make this drastic changeover, the company took everything into consideration and thought through its plans very carefully. They decided to advertise that the new system eliminated rust and sales associated with re-used drums. Further capitalizing on the African love of bathing soap, they set up soap bar giveaways to mammy wagons (buses and produce trucks owned and operated by local women) and drivers at their gas stations, especially the mammies selling kerosene in two-gallon cans. As Dad said, the usual African soap is a long bar called *key soap*. There are almost no bar soaps in the market that Africans can afford, so the company contracted with the African company U.A.C., better known as Lever Brothers. (In West Africa, they control a huge portion of the palm oil trade from the growers, selling everything back to their own chain of Kingsway stores.) Dad's company contracted U.A.C. to make up hotel-size soap bars, wrapped in covers with the company logo (the flying red horse) and the words "Mobil — the clean gasoline." The company ordered enough soap to give away one to every car, truck, lorry, and mammy wagon in the country. These are stored in a warehouse until the campaign is to begin. They cost the company about one pence each (i.e., about 1.4 cents).

Immediately there follows the only reported drought in Ghana's history. There is no water for the people's usual bathing. WaWa.

The company cleaned its tankers and trucked water in for the people's needs. Meanwhile, the free soap disappeared almost completely and re-appeared in the marketplaces, where it sold for three pence. Bad *ju-ju* for Mobil.

NOVEMBER 30, 1955

My father comes home and announces we will be moving to Kumasi, 250 miles to the north. All of us will have to move. Only the small boy and the night watchman will stay. Everyone else will have to move; even Zilbare, his cold poached eggs, his three children, and his wife.

The inventory includes five Coughlans, two gardeners, one cook, his wife, and his three children, two stewards, six puppies with their nursing mother, two Siamese cats, the chickens, the peahens, and everybody's possessions. We rent three mammy wagons, which are distinguished by having no rear lights, not even reflectors. They are even painted distinctively in different colors and have signs on the back like, "Jesus Saves" or "I Walk Alone," each according to its owner's choice.

Samuel and Dad will later find out something about this lack of rear lights or reflectors when on a trip they will take in the upcountry:. Dad and Samuel run right into the back of a mammy wagon and Samuel loses his front teeth. Dad offers to pay for his front teeth, but Samuel takes the money instead to give to his family for a business he is starting.

KUMASI

The road to Kumasi is black tarmac, winding through cocoa farms and jungle patches on either side. Reed and I sing songs we have made up, out of the windows in the spirit of the adventure. It is a long but worthwhile trip. Our new house is bigger than the previous one. The garden has pineapples, tangerines, banana, and orange groves. The building has four bedrooms, a second floor, and a large veranda in the front.

Reed, Coagie, and I call, "Puppies, puppies, puppies," and they arrive in a group of nine or ten, slipping and sliding across the polished veranda to lick our legs and face. Sometimes their sharp little teeth will us to sit up suddenly. Often they chase the Siamese cats to the top of the refrigerator. In the garden, they chase the wild pigeons living on the roof.

Since there are wild pigeons, I decide that if we can get some tame pigeons, we can double our pigeon population by feeding all of them and then pulling out the wild pigeons' feathers so they will stay. They all do. Dad gets Zilbare to get some pigeons, and Isefu builds a pigeon condominium for them on the side of the compound. Every pigeon has his own apartment. This is

33

fine, except that I grow so fond of all the pigeons that I cannot part with any of them, and they become pets rather than tasty dinners.

But puppies grow up, so I have to give them away (or rather, Dad does), all but the one that I named Shadow because he follows me everywhere, and I think he can be as invisible to anyone else as one's own shadow is in the sunlight. In addition, the older he gets, the faster and more graceful he becomes, just like clouds racing in front of the sun.

Soon after, it is Christmas, and Dad brings home a white, putty-nosed monkey. Reed likes to tease it with a stick, — and so, it likes to bite him. I use a different strategy. When it bites me the first time, I bite it back, showing it that I have bigger teeth and can, if I want to, bite back even harder. We are close friends afterward, and go everywhere together. Often riding on bumpy roads on my bike, Monkmonk, as I call him, hangs on to my red curly hair, so I have to go slowly. Though he loves fruit, he is not above climbing trees and eating baby birds. I do think Monkmonk enjoys bicycle riding the best. He rides on my shoulders and hangs on to my curly red hair. He loves those trips. He looks purposefully as though he knows where we are going.

Monkmonk hates baths. He screams bloody murder when he is in the water, but afterwards, he is in heaven: wrapped in a towel, gently placed under my mother's hair dryer, and then brushed and powdered, he is in total heaven. Monkmonk has another passion, and that is flowers. In our neighborhood, we have a man called the flower man, whose only job is to bring and arrange flowers in people's houses. Monkmonk loves this man; unfortunately, the feeling is not mutual. Every time Monkmonk is loose, he goes up a long curtain and wait until the flower man has set up a nice arrangement. Then, at rapid speed, he steals the whole bunch, proceed to eat the flowers he likes, and then throws the rest away.

This drives the poor man almost to quitting until we restrain Monkmonk in a special house. Of course, Monkmonk is always getting out or needing to be rescued from his chain, which we have to use because he breaks everything else. But the whole thing is temporary. Monkmonk learns to leave the flowers alone, and the flower man lowers his standards concerning our house.

Monkmonk also likes naps; he naps in my bed, that is. Whether he is clean or dirty, he likes to lie down under the covers with me, with his brown head and white putty nose on the pillow and close his eyes. During the daytime, his concentration around naps is not long. His eyes pop open as if he remembers something, and he runs off suddenly. At night, he curls himself up and his tail into a ball, then he places his white putty nose and face near my ear and sleeps until the time the birds get up, and then he is off for his day's activities. Monkmonk gets along well with guests, particularly in the evening, when he tries out their drinks. Some drinks he likes, others he doesn't. He does not get along with the puppies, which he can take or leave. As for the pigeons, he likes to pull their feathers, if he can catch them.

Our reputation in the neighborhood, through the flower man, is a little weird, but a number of incidents make it even more so. One night, as our night watchman is sleeping in front of the main door to the house, thieves invade. They came to break in, and not seeing the sleeping night watchman, they stepped on him in front of the door. He let out a great shout, and, in a panic, one of the thieves shot him in the leg.

Later, my father went to visit the watchman in the hospital, and asked what this had taught him. He said, "From now on, master, I will not sleep in front of the door." My father felt that this is not quite the answer he wanted, so one night after drinks on the veranda, my father convinced the night watchman to let him borrow his poison arrows and bow. My father then gave the night watchman a tuppence, a small coin with a hole in it. The man became quite nervous. My father told him to step back some distance towards the banana grove. Then my father told the man to throw the coin in the air. When the night watchman did that, he dove onto the ground. My father, meanwhile, shot the arrow right through the tuppence. Needless to say, our reputation spread through the compounds of Kumasi and the villages around it.

My mother has her role in these matters too. Dad has insisted on buying a car, a Humber Hawk. We have a series of them that never start properly, until Mother figures out the secret. Usually, we all pile in (Dad being at work) and try to start the car. This never works, until my mother announces in a loud voice that we are not going to use the car that day anyway. So then we have to go all the way back into the house. Then we all come out, and the car starts up fine, and goes anywhere we want. Some people in the neighborhood think this has to do with the fact that my father has powerful *ju-ju*, and that this is my mother's version. I just think that the cars are no good.

DECEMBER 14, 1955

My father's friend, the Assumaja-Hene, the warrior chief of the Ashanti nation, has made my father the *Mobilhini* of Kumasi, which means that he is officially installed as a local chief. As my father in later years told us, the Ashanti people are a matriarchal society, so the bloodlines are through the mother. The Ashanti Queen Mother has a strong influence in all affairs. The Ashanti are not conquered, as are some other tribes; they fought the British to a standstill around 1910 and then agreed to a treaty. Mom once said this is probably because they are a matriarchal society.

Dad told us of his first meeting with the Assumaja-Hene, whom he describes as having a blend of the old and the new Ashanti ways. "He came to my office and having been announced by my secretary, stood on one foot, his other resting on his calf. After an interval, he asked, 'Do they have schools for wives in England or the U.S.?' I asked, 'What kind of schools?' The chief asked, 'Does your wife see to it that there is a good meal ready for you at noon and in the evening?' The chief has a new, young wife who is not overly impressed by her husband's status and it is clear that he hopes that my father could suggest a solution. All he can say is that all husbands are in the same boat, but that all things considered, we are both lucky." The Assumaja-Hene and his wife Catherine become fast friends of my parents.

The ceremony, cocktail party, and dinner for Dad's installment as *Mobilhini* of Kumasi are the events of the year. Dad and Mom receive two mahogany stools, symbolizing the male and female spirits of the Ashanti nation. What I remember most is that Reed and I have to wear matching white shorts and long socks and how I want to be able to wear long pants, like the grown-up men.

DECEMBER 15, 1955

My mother's eyeglasses are stolen in Kumasi. She is concerned because it will take six months to replace them. At the time, the house is being painted, so we have about forty painters plus the household staff. They have one song they sing all day, at different cadences, and that is "alleluvia, alleluvia, alleluvia." My parents thought this is a local chant; actually alleluvia is an English word that means, to paint. Anyway, because my parents are friends with the Assumaja-Hene, he recommends a witch doctor be called to help with the eyeglasses. Glasses are a sign of respect in West Africa because Europeans use them, so they became a sign of fashion for the Africans.

My brother and I are quite excited by this prospect. So, on the appointed day, a black Cadillac limousine arrives, and out steps a man in his thirties, in a well-tailored suit. In an impeccable Oxford accent, he asks if Madame is in. She is. So he arranges to interview everyone in the garage. He must've had quite a reputation, because it goes very quiet around the house. The *ju-ju* man lights a small charcoal brazier in the garage. Then he has the painters and staff line up. He then asks if they have stolen the glasses. When they say, "No," he withdraws a small, metal stick from the fire and touches their tongues. Quite scientific, actually, since the guilty one will have a dry tongue. After half an hour, he comes back to say that not only did he know who took the glasses, but they have also been broken as well. The thief is one of the household staff. Since he cannot return the glasses, he does not charge her.

My mother does not believe the *ju-ju* man, but about a month later, she finds Abel (the first steward) wearing her school ring, which he claims he found in the garden.

DECEMBER 16, 1955

West Africa has its own way. My parents are members of a golf club, but playing golf is not simple. Besides having a caddy, you hire "anti-crow" people who scare off the crows that will swoop down and steal golf balls, thinking they are eggs to eat. WaWa.

What I do not know about the anti-crow people (and my father does), is that the people hired to keep the crows away are called fore-caddies, who also serve to watch where the tee shots and fairway shots go. His favorite is particularly good at finding Dad's errant drives into the rough. Using his prehensile toes, he can stand straight up in full view of Dad's opponent and give Dad a superior lie. Meanwhile, using only his toes, he will tee up Dad's golf ball so well that when Dad arrives, it is a good lie and gives Dad an improved chance of recovery. Naturally, he helps my dad's partner, and no doubt the opponent's fore-caddy does the same. In any case, the caddies improve their tips considerably.

My father's *ju-ju* does not always work. He is once playing golf with two priests and another partner, with the usual number of anti-crow people. He and his partner are doing very well. They are winning every hole. But from the beginning of the game, one priest remarked what a nice hat my father has, and how my father's hat will make a good gift for his monsignor. But my father really loves his hat. Finally, since he and his partner are doing so well at every hole, he agrees at the last hole to wager his hat on that hole. Unfortunately, the priest wins that hole, and my father has to give up the hat, which he misses to this day. WaWa.

DECEMBER 17.–21, 1955

Since Coagie is younger, his whereabouts are supposed to be known at all times, at least between Mother and Teresa, the nanny. One day, neither Mother nor Teresa knows where Coagie is. The whole house goes into a total alert (or panic, depending upon your point of view). Everyone, including the watchman, the flower man, and the gardener go to check the neighboring compounds. Since there are so many, Mother simply tells them to keep going until they find him, or to call back when they do. Reed and I are out on our bikes to add to the crew. For two hours, nobody can find him. Reed and I circle the area numerous times and are unable to spot him. We are exhausted. Mother has sent for Dad...Only the worst seems possible. Finally, the miracle occurs:. Coagie arrives home safe and sound. The nanny next door, with the twins, had put Coagie in the middle of the stroller, and all three have gone to sleep with the top down. So it is assumed she is just taking the twins for a stroll. She had seen people rushing about, but she is on the main promenade. No one had thought to ask her a thing. Coagie is quite refreshed from his nap, and everyone vows to think of that possibility next time if they cannot find him. After all, Coagie is friends with the twins. WaWa.

WILLIAM COUGHLAN JR.

I used to engage in ant wars. I use large, shiny, yellowish-brown clicker ants because of the sound they make and collect them in big bottles. Then I break open the large castle-like termite mounds and wait until the termite soldiers emerge. It soon becomes clear that my clickers could only temporarily win against the termites. In frustration, I borrow garden tools from Isefu to dig at the bottom of the mound. During the day I dig, but they re-appear at night. Thinking myself clever, I buy a box of cherry bombs, which I plant after all my work. Sure enough, in the morning, the ants partially covered up the bombs. Unfortunately, blowing up wet, reconstructed tunnels does not do much damage. Finally, a group of convicts who work in the field behind the house decide to show me what there is an anthill, by digging five feet down to the queen termite in her special hardened house. That temporarily ends my interest in the ant wars, since the queen has a small head that is connected to a large, ugly, yellow sack of termite eggs several inches long.

My father has a 100 percent American entrepreneurial streak. When he calculates how many shillings we are spending per egg for the kitchen, he decides to turn Abel, our first steward, into a chicken farmer (or at least make Abel rich in this lucrative business). He commissions a virtual chicken palace for the back of the compound. Six workmen build an elevated chicken house, so the rain will not wash it away. Each chicken has its own apartment, the fence posts are deeply planted, and there is a full-sized chicken gate. The chicken wire is buried in the ground.

The chickens, scientifically tested and selected, are flown in, met by workmen at the airport, and taken to their new chicken palace. No expense is spared on their grain, either. Zilbare puts in his scrawny West African chickens as well. Unfortunately, one of them has drooping sickness, which causes chickens' necks to droop, and when they can't reach the grain, they die of starvation.

40

Unfortunately, these American chickens are not tested against drooping sickness, and about half of them die. "Never mind you mind"; my father still says we will make a profit per egg, anyway.

Well, the chickens grow up, but there is no egg production. The news is out in the garden, and a local green snake is helping itself to the eggs. But one day, he swallows a big American egg, and gets caught in the fence, and Isefu dispatches him. Now, my father is sure that we will have eggs, expensive by now, but he doesn't count on soldier ant season. Soldier ants march in columns, until you mess with them, and then they use guerrilla tactics.

Our American chickens think the ants' columns are things to eat. That is fine for the first hundred thousand ants; after that, the tables turn, and in the morning, when we come out, we find five mounds of ants where there have been five chickens, with one chicken standing on the roof. It is so traumatized by the whole episode that it never again lays a single egg.

That doesn't stop Reed and me from formulating our revenge. First we hook up the hose and flood out the banana grove and the chicken coop. This does not stop the waterlogged ants from biting us too. So after our father has left for work, we take a large barrel of oil and light the whole mess on fire. But the ants keep piling on, and finally by their sheer weight and numbers, they smother the blaze. The neighborhood gossips about the crazy Americans. WaWa.

Eventually, my brother and I have to go to school. This time, we go to an integrated army school in Kumasi. I have a girlfriend named Jean, and she and I play together during recess. One day, the schoolyard bully starts picking on me. He is bigger and stronger than I am. I run to avoid him, but he is faster and more agile. Finally, he gets me into a corner near a fence, sits on my chest, and hits me on the face. I give him a solid burst of crocodile tears and he goes away boasting of his conquest.

Jean comes to me to me and asks, "Why did you do that?"

"Well," I said, "I gave him what he wanted, and now he will not bother me again."

I wonder why girls do not know about these things or whether she seriously thinks I am going to risk life and limb for a common bully. My younger brother Reed used to call me a bully until I got so angry that I hit him and then he runs to Mom. I have not forgotten that Bucky Lybolt and I have excluded Reed when we were younger. So, I think I know a bit about this bully business. Am I really a coward? Or do I need more powerful *ju–ju?*

After school, we splash and swim short distances in a concrete water tank that is connected to the roof. Dad had the top broken in and the broken parts of the roof made into a concrete platform, so the pool is half shallow and half deep. Reed and I offer swimming lessons to Zilbare's oldest two pickens— even though we can't swim. We do not drown, because Isefu the gardener keeps the water level low. None of us does more than the usual choking, peeing, and spitting up in the water tank.

My brother Reed and I have our own bedroom when we live in Kumasi, but unlike Accra, there are no roaring air conditioners here. Instead we have mosquito netting around each bed. One evening, while my parents are busy having a cocktail party on the veranda, we discover a bat trapped on the netting in our bedroom. Reed and I jump back and forth, throwing pillows, while the bat flies around the bedroom. At first, the bat evades us easily, but after a while it is slower to respond. We begin to throw the pillows faster and jump harder on our beds. Then Reed crashes off one of the beds head-first, with a loud yell.

"Are you all right?" I ask. He holds up his arm and shows me that his wrist is bent like a pretzel.

We both worry that we will be in trouble. Reed is too frightened to cry. I argue with him that he has to go downstairs. Finally, he goes down to Mom but comes back in a few minutes. "Mom says to stop showing off," he says. I convince him to go see Dad. He goes downstairs again and shows Dad his bent wrist. Now, it is true that Dad had won a Naval Cross in World War II, but when he takes one look at Reed's wrist, he faints.

The cocktail party comes to a halt as Dad is revived and Reed is whisked off to the hospital with Samuel, the driver, and Mom. Meanwhile, fortunately for me, only Teresa, the nanny, comes to see what had happened. She kills the bat with a broom, and to my relief, she tells me that Reed has been taken to the hospital.

Reed becomes such a frequent visitor to the hospital that he has his own bed reserved for him. We both go for malaria for two months, and in addition to that, Reed goes for an ear infection. Then there is the case of the unknown tropical disease Reed contracted that caused him to have difficulty breathing properly. He is taken to the hospital for that and the doctor who examines him is not only unable to diagnose the disease, she catches it herself— and is reported to have left the country as a consequence. WaWa.

When Reed and I are brought home from the hospital after our bouts with malaria, Mom serves us frozen strawberries that have been flown in with someone coming from Accra. These strawberries have been brought from Kingsway in Accra just for us. I think they are great because they appear to be big, as big as watermelons. Since then, if I have a high fever, I get a desire for strawberries or a vision of large strawberries first. Perhaps it is just that I remember those beautiful, scrumptious strawberries.

My brother's luck in Kumasi continues to get him hospital visits. One day, he and Isefu are trimming the hedges. They share the top steps of the stepladder. Isefu is trimming the hedge with the shears, while Reed is brushing leaves off behind him. Reed is more enthusiastic and faster, so he accidentally catches his hand in the shears. What is at hand, so to speak, gets trimmed. Poor Reed has to have many stitches. His ju-ju in Kumasi is not *fine-fine past Takoradi self.*

Life in Kumasi is also lived on the veranda in the evenings. There are many stories I remember my parents and their guests telling. Sometimes they talk about lions dragging people out of villages. But what sticks in my memory is one guest's explanation of elephants. During the mango season, the elephants eat so many mangos that the fruit ferments in their stomachs, and they get drunk and tear up villages. And when they're hung over, they are even more destructive.

If elephants are a problem, baboons are an organized menace. Baboons go on the ground in military formations. Even lions avoid them. If they think a village has been interfering with what they want to do, they throw stones and sticks and march into the village in a triangular formation with the meanest, strongest baboons at the points of the triangle. Then they jump up on the roofs of the villages and systematically take the roofs off. They are very strong, and compared to an occasional elephant, are quite the local newsmakers. I say "local news," because the local news travels by the drumming between the villages in the bush until it reaches the more urban areas, where it gets reported by newspapers or by people traveling through the guest houses up-country (a place I am never quite sure where it is because people further "up-country" from us will often refer to others further up-country from them as "up-country.").

DECEMBER 22 TO--23, 1955

Every Saturday and Sunday, Hausa traders come by to sell their wares. It is a treat for my brother and me, because we act as translators. The most prized pieces are solid ebony carved heads, which went go for $35 to $45. Each piece starts at an outrageous price and then goes down until the trader swears that the price will ruin his family. Sometimes we buy; sometimes he packs the items back up.

Sometimes after Reed and I have a long translation from pidgin back to English for our parents (or whoever might be visiting on the veranda with them), I wonder if maybe what the Hausa traders have said is true: this trade is ruining their families, because they cannot bring more items than what they carry on their heads, and if they do not sell their wares at the right price, what will happen to the Hausa and their families? Will they be *yacatti* (finished)?

DECEMBER 24–TO-25, 1955

At Christmas time in Kumasi, marching bands and African dancers in outfits of paper -mâché and straw march through our driveway. This is their way of celebrating Christmas. My father takes films of this, but often he forgets to take his thumb out of the way, so we have many home movies of close-ups of his thumb.

Dad (or I should say, "Santa Claus") gets me something special for Christmas, a terrific present. I have no idea where he got it, or where he got the idea. But it is perfect for Reed's and my unsuccessful battles with the ants. It is perfect for someone who has tortured the insects, someone who even feels guilty about shooting down hummingbirds, and killing the poor bat in our bedroom antics. It is a butterfly collection in a two-sided velvet-lined wooden box. Of course, each one is dead, but beautiful in death, pinned in place through the wings and body and each in a different- colored mosaic. Each a variety of size laid out in the symmetry to compensate for their different sizes by the brightness of their colors. The box is thin and simple, and as fragile as the butterflies. But on the occasions I show it off, it never draws less than full attention from adults; it is beautiful. It is a wonderful present. WaWa for Dad and Santa.

Unfortunately, due to the import agricultural laws of the United States, I have to leave it behind. I wish I had it to brighten up a gray New England winter day. Even the most pretentious adult, only trying to take a brief glance, cannot help peering at and soaking up the beauty of the flies of multi-color, as I remember them now.

Sometimes at night, even at Christmas, we hear the bombs going off between the two warring factions as independence grows near. Our British friends never broke their conversations. On certain days, it is not safe to go to the Zongo meat market.

DECEMBER 27, 1955

Three people die (or I think they died), in Kumasi, and make an impression on me. It is not as though I am unaware that people are dying in the bombing by the National Liberation Movement (NLM) and the CCCP (this acronym was I think the one the northern tribal's used for their party) — the two parties warring for political control of Ghana's independence — but there are three understandings of the matter. The Africans (depending on whom you talked to) deplore it, it made them look foolish or worried that it will delay independence. Other Africans, who are partisans, acted as though it is a given that their side will win and treat the bombings like soccer match scores. Then there is the British theory: "The natives are restless." This seems to indicate that the worse side of every belief, worry, attitude, or understanding, is true of the Africans. My parents think the bombings are a problem.

To this day, I'm not exactly sure whether I dreamed this or saw it. It's hazy in my mind. Maybe I don't want to know or remember.

A dream or not, it changes my vision of what a crowd may or may not do in a riot. Samuel, Mother, Reed, and I go shopping in the Zongo meat market, the market connected not only to the general market of Kumasi, but also where demonstrations of the various factions and parties marched on their own and against others.

Samuel comes to Mom and says, "We dey go now, Madame. Trouble I dey not know here to be."

As we get into the car to leave, I look out of the back window. I know I have an image of two groups of people waving sticks and machetes at each other. A medium-built man without any stick or machete stands frozen between the two groups. As the two groups crowd into direct contact with each other, I catch sight of the man clutching his loincloth as he begins to fall towards the ground. My imagination takes over as a tunnel of vision out of the rear window of the car. It remains with me to this day as I see the sticks and machetes rain down on him.

To compare any death with any other is, back then, a matter of degrees of fear. I think the world is supposed to have justice, and if certain matters are in place or in evidence, then possibly there are things you can do to stop or prevent death.

The Greek company man, Mr. Kadis, has been in the hospital ward opposite Reed's reserved bed and my bed. He is friendly and has been tolerant when we have a lot of pain due to our ear infections and have to yell about it. He is still there when we leave the hospital. When we get home, I overhear Mom and Dad talking. "Mr. Kadis isn't getting better. They expect he will die soon. It's a pity. He is so young and has a wife and a child back in Greece." When Reed and I get upstairs, I say nothing to Reed, but I vow that if the matter gets worse, then I will fix it by praying to

God so hard that God will intervene. For the next two nights, I lay awake for up to three hours and pray to God. But by now, what is *probable* begins to be predicted as *inevitable*. So I vow to make sure God hears me. Maybe there have been too many other messages for God to have time to hear me to do anything the night before. The night before Mr. Kadis is predicted to die, I stay up all night praying. First I sing every hymn I know of, which mostly are my own versions, since I can't remember how they go, without the organ or the others singing. Then I begin to beg God with lists of reasons why I think this man is a good man and God ought to save him. This man is a good man. I keep this up until the early hours before dawn and fall asleep in the middle of the list of reasons. Mr. Kadis dies the next day, and his body is flown back to Greece for his funeral. This dampens my enthusiasm for miracles.

JANUARY 1, 1956

There is the case of the pregnant French woman who is walking down the road with her husband, who is on the inside lane to the oncoming traffic. A cab comes along and knocks her two hundred feet down the road, and the driver runs off in the bush and is never caught. The husband is unharmed, but the pregnant woman and baby die. I overhear that discussion from the veranda, too, and I am shocked. It is obvious to me there is no justice in this matter, so it makes no sense to me that the whole matter is discussed by everybody, and in such detail, especially until they notice me, and then the topic is changed. *Why do adults do that?* I think. *There is no point.* WaWa.

JANUARY 2, 1956

Samuel lets Mother know what days are safe to go to the Zongo meat market. The American Ambassador, who is a black man, ignores the warning of a bad day in the Zongo area. His chauffeured car gets caught in the middle of a riot, and both sides think he is some third party come to interfere with what they are doing, so they nearly overturn and burn his car. However, the police rescue him, recognizing the American flag flying on his car. Our British friends think it is typically American. WaWa.

JANUARY 3, 1956

According to Dad, during the troubled times in Kumasi, he and Mom get invited to a dance at the Queensway Hotel downtown. Mr. Moore, another executive, is staying at the company guesthouse on company business from Accra, and is also invited.

Samuel, the driver, picks up Dad, Mom, and then Mr. Moore. They are driven to the hotel entrance. Samuel opens the doors for them to get out. There, directly in front of them, is a man who appears to be shot dead.

Dad turns to Samuel and says, "I thought you say this man have too much *Ju-ju* to get shot."

Samuel says, "But, master, this man, he be knifed from the back."

"Ah-ha," says Dad, and he steps over the man.

Mom lifts up her long dress and steps over the man too. Mr. Moore, following gingerly, also steps over the man. Then all three of them get a table near the palm tree that is thick, large, and in the middle of the courtyard of the Queensway. On all four sides of the palm tree there are posters in English that say, "Political discussion is strictly prohibited." The dance begins, and Dad and Mom quite enjoy themselves. Mr. Moore leaves early from the dance and early the next day for Accra. Samuel has to make an extra trip for Mr. Moore through the dangerous Zongo area and then returns to pick up my Dad and Mom. Mr. Moore does not return to Kumasi as long as Dad and Mom are there.

Our annual leave comes up. My parents, taking advantage of a circuitous route, decide to stop off in Rome, Paris, London, and New York. Oddly enough, when we went get to Rome, we look for a restaurant that specializes in American food. I have an especially strong craving for a vanilla shake, so while we are in Rome, we boys eat nothing but French fries, hamburgers, and drink milkshakes.

MARCH 2, 1956

The Coliseum looks like the underneath of termite castles I have partially dug out in Kumasi. The major difference is that the tunnels are human-sized, and the termites have not built such a symmetrical artifice. I begin to imagine a sandy floor in the sunshine with a cheering crowd of Romans in colored togas, like African cloth. I imagine seeing Gladiators, Christians, and lions, some in the tunnels below the sandy floor and some on the top. I have only one question: Did they use lady lions or male lions? Lady lions do all the work, I hear. It is always they who jump out of the bush and drag people away to feed their families. That's what they say on the veranda in Kumasi. Male lions with families just wait to be waited upon. Young male lions go around together, it is true, but they have no beards like the lions with families, so I think they won't be as attractive to the crowds. Maybe you can starve a male lion so that he can eat a gladiator or a Christian, and maybe it will have a beard, or rather, a mane, but it seems uncertain to me. Then I realize it has been a while since they did these things, so I keep the matter to myself. WaWa, lions.

The other thing that stands out in my mind about Rome are the museums. It is not so much what is in them but how long the corridors are. Most of the people in the paintings look old and serious. I remember a guide proudly announcing that each corridor is a quarter of a mile long. My legs seem too short for such long corridors, yet my parents feel I am old enough to appreciate it all. So I did do a lot of walking. It is, as Dad later remembers, one of the thirteen Vatican Museums.

MARCH 7, 1956

We fly to Paris, where my parents come down with malaria from not taking their quinine. My youngest brother, Coagie, has never seen a bidet, so he goes to the bathroom in it. My parents think it is funny. I am more interested in the pinball machines. In France, you need to be seventeen to play, but the hotelkeeper lets us play anyway even though I am ten and Reed is eight. When Reed and I get tired of pinball, we decide to go exploring, and we get a note in French from the hotelkeeper explaining where the hotel is. After a few blocks, we get completely lost, so we go to the nearest policeman, but he doesn't know either. The three of us proceed to investigate nearly every shop in the neighborhood. After ten or twelve shops, the gendarme finds out that the hotel is right behind him, near the square where he directs traffic. After that, we hang around the hotel and play pinball. It seems no one knows where they are in Paris. Wa Wa

Even though my parents are sick, they do manage a tour of Paris, including a boat trip down the Seine. First, we have a Continental breakfast: fresh rolls, pastries, and as a special treat, a hot Swiss chocolate so sweet, it tastes like melted sugar in a bath of lightly creamed chocolate. There is sugar everywhere! From every bite of the treats to every sip of drink, Reed and I have three rounds of hot chocolate before we are ready to leave, since the 'rents have taken Coagie upstairs to get him ready for the trip.

A small tour auto-bus pulls up to the hotel. Nobody except our family gets on at our hotel, since no other foreign tourists are staying there. I like this because the American tourists wear Hawaiian print shirts, talk in loud voices, and everyone stares at them as much as they gawk and point while taking pictures of everything. Of course, those tourists would get on later. They embarrass me, so I drag my parents to the back of the bus, where we are safe from the glaring eyes of the Parisians and the tourists.

We see a number of statues and squares before finally seeing the Arc de Triumph. We pass under the Eiffel Tower and double back to the Seine where we all unload to get on a two-tier tour boat of the river. What I notice on the trip, are the cafés. They are everywhere — cafés at corners, mid-blocks, half inside the buildings. Cafés seem to be where everybody in Paris is, at least from 8 a.m. to 10 a.m. I wonder if the Parisians take a nap in the afternoon the way everyone but the working Europeans do in Africa. If so, when do they get to work? Maybe they are all so rich that they do not have to, except for the police and those who work in hotels and I assume, cafés. The traffic is terrible: buses, cars, motorbikes, and motorcycles with and without sidecars are everywhere. They have to be going somewhere, but my wondering stops at the quiet of the river. My parents warn Reed and me that this trip is for both French lunch and French dinner. We get a table on the upper deck with a good view. The tour boat slowly moves into the river's murky water. A shudder passes through the boat as it picks up speed and starts going, but soon, the pounding of the engine slows to a dull beat. After a while, it is hard to tell whether the boat is moving slower or faster than the brown water of the Seine.

Food to us is African curry or hamburgers, hot dogs, French fries and a shake, but French food turns out to be quite different. Everything comes to the table covered in a sauce. Sometimes you can see what is underneath, but mostly, you cannot tell. At first, I think it is a necessary method, just to get us children to eat our lunch. It tastes fine, but the only problem is that the portions are fit for a bird. Speaking of which, I have thought I have seen small birds eaten in Africa, but the one I see on my plate seemed the limit. So I ask Dad to ask what it is. "A thrush," says the waiter. *Quite French*, I think to myself. These Parisians may be very rich, but they have to eat sparrows? How sad; maybe they are not so well off after all! Mom puts it aside in favor of her kindness to animals. Reed and I try it out, but we are still hungry. It is sweet and crunchy but not enough to fill us up. Finally, Dad asks the waiter if they have any American food. The waiter turns sour, but says he will bring something. Twenty minutes later, four perfectly medium- rare steaks appear, but again, they are not big enough for birds. So I conclude that French cooking is great for breakfast, but for a hungry lunch, tasty but small. WaWa, French cooking.

Reed and I spend the afternoon watching the water roll under the boat. Then a broad-shouldered tourist with a Hawaiian shirt and white hairy legs asks Reed and me, "Do you all want to see the gargoyles?" My mind races. This man is from Texas — I have no doubt. But I am too old to ask if he knows Pancho and Cisco or the Lone Ranger and Tonto, who (or so I believed when I was younger) most certainly, lived in Texas.

Trying to be polite, I ask, "Are Mr. and Mrs. Gargoyle from Texas?"

He laughs so hard, I think he will fall off the boat. I cannot figure out what he thinks is so funny. In Africa, I have learned that strange names can definitely be somebody's name.

"No, son," he explains, "the gargoyles are on the cathedrals, and you can see them through my binoculars."

"No, thanks," I say, feeling stupid and embarrassed.

But Reed says he will, and after his enthusiasm, I change my mind and take a look at the next cathedral. There they are — ugly, gray, stone masks grinning into the afternoon sky. After that, Reed and I return to the table, running around and around it until we are ordered to sit down and have some more hot chocolate. Coagie screams and yells when Reed and I leave the table, but when we come back, he is napping.

Soon it is evening, and the captain turns on the colored lights, reminding me of a circus that Dad and Mom have taken us to. When Reed was two years old and I was only four, they had taken us to a circus in Liberty, New York. , and there had been an announcement: "the elephants are coming, and children are to move to the back of the tent!". Reed and I got up and began to follow orders, while the 'rents found the whole matter quite humorous. WaWa.

Dad and Mom go over to the railing to watch the couples walking along the promenade by the river and under the bridges. They return as dinner begins in the darkening evening. Mom says it is all very romantic. I ask what does that have to do with the word *romantic* in the museum in Rome. I have an idea— those paintings definitely suggest nude women and men doing something "romantic." I know Dad has once explained the whole matter to me once when I was in the second grade, and I told the twins, Mary and Kathy, and my best girlfriend Joanne Angle. Of course, they told their parents, and their parents called my teacher, and I must wait after school for my parents to pick me up. I do not think I got it right back then, because I told my girlfriends something about telephone poles and tomatoes. I was only waiting for a better explanation, and Dad says, "Well, *romance* is something you find out about when you are a teenager, and the *romantic* is something about art history, and you find out about that in college." So we return to the hotel and leave for London the next day.

MARCH 9, 1956

In London, the hotel is much bigger (the beds are excellent to jump back and forth between when our parents aren't looking). But there is one good thing and one bad thing about the place. At lunch and supper, there is a vast choice of desserts to pick from. The bad thing is that when my parents go to look for schools for us in England, they hire a nanny, who is a witch. She is nasty, strict, mean, and stingy, and unpleasant in her looks. I think my parents thought she would keep us in line. I think they are right.

MARCH 10, 1956

Then comes what we are all looking forward to on our trip to New York. Somehow Dad has arranged passage for all of us on the *Neiue Amsterdam* back to New York — first class, no less. First we take an English train to Southampton with compartments, a whole compartment to ourselves. It is night when we arrive. Then we go to the ship, which looks like a floating skyscraper, with decks and decks of lights going up.

Reed and I have our own cabin, and we soon memorize all the decks and cabin numbers. We children are organized into one group so parents can find us and not have us be all over the ship. We have endless parties, cakes, and tugs-of-war and ping-pong tournaments. The ping- pong tournaments are the best, because you never know when the ship will roll, and you knock the ball into the ocean. The trip lasts about a week, during which time it goes rough just on the night when it is our turn to have the dessert we want. On that night, every table in the first- class dining room, takes their turn to order something special for dessert. Dad and Mom have ordered baked Alaska. Unfortunately, Reed and I are too green to eat any, and have to retire to bed early.

The boat arrives at night. It is late, and the stevedores are surly, but I have a distinct feeling that things are not the same. It is as if I have landed in a strange country. Apart from the ugliness of the area, it feels cold and inhuman. WaWa.

Feelings are funny, but somehow, they are still the best indicators of change. I have gone away and come back, I think, the same. But in the following days, when we are to move to Luago Gate in Baimville, I notice some clues based on WaWa in my own terms.

I am no longer comfortable with American adults. They do not seem to be sincerely interested in me as the Africans have been. For example, my sixth-grade teacher, although she knows I have been living in West Africa, never asks me about it. Also, I am upset that I am treated as a child and not as a little adult. Strangely, adults do not act as though they love children here. People seem to feel there is something wrong with the variety of people in Africa, that diversity itself is somehow suspected. The messages are subtle but deep.

MARCH 13, 1956

Back in the United States Luago Gate is a wonderful world to retreat into. Luago is a farmhouse with a pond and a large snapping turtle. On the other hand, school is an event that mainly means taking half an hour to comb my hair just right, trade bubble- gum cards, and be champion at dodge ball. But it is boring, because I have soon read every book in the classroom except the spelling books, and there is no school library. Occasionally, there are bomb alerts. Our desks are the sort that can be set up in different positions for reading, writing, and so on; these have to be flattened during practice raids, with glasses and ties on the inside. So I look forward to returning to Luago Gate. There I sit on my favorite fishing rock and catch sunfish (only to throw them back). When

I am not doing that, I have a flotilla of small metal boats. You put a candle inside them, and the water will go through the small internal boiler, making the boat go putt-putt-putt, propelling it along the water. These can go for hours. In the summer, there is the wild raspberry patch to where my brother and I would help ourselves.

The main character in the pond is a snapping turtle that is as big as my arms are round. Once he decides to leave the pond and my mother calls the state police, but he escapes over a wall before the trooper arrives. Another time, I drop a rock on him in the pond as big as he is, but he just disappears. Of course, I try cherry bombs, but to no effect. But as the summer wears on, I begin to see what the snapping turtle must have been living on. There is a colony of eels under my fishing rock. By accident, I catch two of them so I give them to our landlady, who says she will cook them. I have heard that they wiggle in the pan, even after you cut off their heads!

JUNE 15, 1956

Dad sends Reed and me to the YMCA summer camp. Reed gets confused and ends up going to the Catholic Church instead of the Protestant one, but his mistake is not half as embarrassing as mine. During the great end-of-summer Capture the Flag games, I forget midway through which team I am really on, so I have to run back and forth avoiding both sides until someone catches me. I surrender only to find out I have surrendered to my own side. WaWa.

JULY 14, 1956

The worst part of this time at Luago Gate is that Dad had let some other boy I didn't know fish in our pond. This boy caught all the sunfish and let them die right next to where he was fishing. I was furious with Dad because there are nothing but eels and tiny sunfish left. And the eels make a mess out of my fishing gear.

JULY 15, 1956

My old friend Bucky Lybolt from Balmville and the woods smoking days begins to show us his new character as a young adult. First, we buy hunting knives. Many hours are spent throwing them at a big tree, to see if we can get them to stick in. We go through quite a few, since we often damage the handles rather than getting the blades in the tree. Then there is his collection of girlie magazines. Once I almost broke my leg on account of these magazines. Bucky and Reed are on one side of the barn, where they can see the house. "Mother is coming!," they tell me. I leap off my perch on the roof, only to find it is a false alarm.

JULY 16, 1956

One Saturday morning, Reed, Coagie, and I are sitting at the breakfast table. Dad has made a breakfast of Eggs Benedict and a huge platter of scrambled eggs surrounded with sausage and bacon. The silence between Dad and Mom had silenced us boys. Dad finally breaks the silence.

"How do you want your eggs, dear?" he asks Mom.

Mom motions for the platter to be passed to her, and taking the platter, she takes aim and throws it right at Dad. Dad stands motionless with eggs, bacon, and sausage dripping all over his face and clothes. Reed, Coagie, and I burst into laughter.

"Go to your rooms now," Dad and Mom say in unison.

WaWa. Adults are odd.

DECEMBER 20, 1956

In the winter, we have the only West African hockey team in our neighborhood, and we do quite well against all comers. But this winter, my father gets reassigned to West Africa. At first, I am excited. I looked forward to more WaWa. But my parents explain that they will first send us (Reed and me) to school in England, and we will visit Africa on vacations when they can afford to send for us.

ENGLAND

JANUARY 10, 1957

Vacations in Copthorne School, our British prep school, are one month at Easter, one month at Christmas, and two months in the summer. Though my father cannot promise he can afford to fly us out every vacation, he says he will try. This temporarily assuages my feelings.

But if Baimville is tough on my WaWa feelings, school in England is of another sort. First of all, there are uniforms: gray shorts, white shirts, knee socks, and big snot rags that will never fit in your pockets (and are always dirty anyway). We are to wear red ties with blue stripes: a regular one for everyday, and a fancier one for Sunday. And there is also the matter of the wool underwear that always seems to appear in the warm months. The rest of the time, we have to cross our legs to stay warm. The best tailor made our jackets, but they always smelled sweaty from having to run to and fro for the seniors.

JANUARY 11, 1957

A world ruled by seniority is not one Reed and I are used to. Even in the United States, it is no sin for people to visit people

60

in other classrooms and meet new people; not so in England. Entry into a forum or classroom is a matter of privilege. When I protest that we believe in democracy, I was physically thrown out. Punishment by the master's ranks in three forms: Latin lines, standing by yourself on a bench, and caning. Latin lines can be a punishment for any one of a variety of infractions, from running in the corridor to not saying what is desired. These are memorized in five to ten lines each. Hardcore people can do twenty at a recitation. Usually it is from Caesar though other texts are used for the hardcore violators who have often already memorized the whole of our portions of the Gallic Wars. Standing on the bench means no one can talk with you, and you have to stand until you are told to get down. Sometimes this happens in classes, and sometimes not. It is very tiring, since you don't know when it will end. I once stood for four hours because I made a weird noise standing in line for morning chapel, and did not confess until after a pointed sermon about telling the truth. I always mumble my lines in a combination of American brogue and pidgin English, so they soon stop giving me that punishment.

Besides the fact that you cannot enter other forums or classes (whether you believe in democracy or not), each forum has a means to control its own members, and that is the pile-on. The pile-on is a punishment where the offender is placed on the floor, and then the heavier boys, then the less heavy boys all the way to the smallest boys in the class will pile on in different directions until everyone in the forum is piled on the offender, and there are no more students to add. Torsos, arms, and legs in all directions, cover the student at the bottom very quickly to maximize its effect. Whoever is on the bottom has that squishy feeling and is short of breath when the pile-on is undone, usually a few minutes before the teachers come in, to investigate the usual yelling and shouting that accompany a pile-on.

JANUARY 18, 1957

Mr. Quesie is the music teacher and in charge of the choir at the chapel.

Mr. Tim is the headmaster and is not fond of Mr. Quesie.

Mr. Tim is large, heavy-set, and bushy- browed. He can scowl like a water buffalo or smile like a general over his troops—, us, his schoolboys. His laugh is hearty and comes from his huge frame.

Mr. Quesie is thin, edgy, and medium-built. He has a light voice, long, thin fingers on delicate, pale hands, and a high-pitched laugh.

Mr. Tim looks good on the school tractor or up on the school pulpit.

Mr. Quesie is a nervous organ player who moves with the music as he plays and can't help singing in the background with his choir. He is a good piano teacher. His system is to number the notes and your fingers together in sequence, as you play from the middle C outward on the piano. We practice many songs over and over again. Unfortunately, I take to memorizing by the number, so I get quite good by the numbers. However, when Mr. Quesie goes to teach me to read the notes directly, my mind is always elsewhere. It is spring, and I want to play lawn tennis and go swimming in the greenish and brackish water of the school swimming pool. I have to be content with swimming every Saturday and Wednesday, which are half- – holidays when we get to play sports instead of studying. Dreams can come true sometimes.

Mr. Tim and Mr. Quesie never see eye-to-eye about the hymns we sing, nor what Mr. Quesie is teaching the choir. Mr. Quesie always plays hymns that the choir can specialize in, sounding pure, sweet, and innocent. Mr. Tim likes those we can all properly belt out together, with Mr. Tim in the lead. Since Mr. Tim is the headmaster, after a while, he fires Mr. Quesie— and now, we have no music teacher. I get my dream for extra swimming and playing lawn tennis. But today, I wish I had learned how to read music and had not been such a daydreamer when I was going to learn swimming and tennis anyway. WaWa to reading music.

JUNE 5, 1957

Swimming has its risqué or more embarrassing side, depending on how you look at it. The two younger matrons in their early twenties are quite attractive, and they have swimming pool duty. We boys get the same thing as we get for our cold baths in the morning — total nudity in front of all!

The older boys—those, ages twelve to thirteen—, use the strategy of running cannonballs aimed at the matrons in case of embarrassment, splashing them with water so that they cannot see the parts of the body in question. Alternatively, diving into the pool at the shallow end works because the water is so green. Hence, staying in the pool is good strategy in case you are embarrassed. Usually, all of that passes in favor of paying as little attention as one can to the women. So I will just swim and enjoy myself, even if I feel self-conscious running naked in front of them.

There is talk in the dorms about certain younger matrons and older boys. In fact, from my dorm, you can hear the younger matrons going upstairs to their rooms, and on occasion unknown others going upstairs too. After lights- out, the older boys discuss sex, and the younger ones just listen in silence. The longer we have been in school, the more elaborate the stories become. Mainly, younger boys want to know how to, while the older boys just make up that they have done it so many times, with the usual bravado of the Don Juan they imagine themselves to be.

(1960 foreshadow) Three years later, still in England, Reed wrote me more about the swimming pool. He, Tom, and George have decided

to go down by the pool just before graduation exercises. It is a sunny day with fluffy, white clouds, and the green hills on the border of Sussex and Surrey are positively verdant in spring. Parents are gathering on the cricket green for the ceremony that marked their sons going on to Winchester, Charter House, Eton, or wherever. The 'rents are not there, so Reed and his friends can sneak off to find something to do. At the pool, they find the headmaster's babysitter taking a nap fully dressed next to the pool. Creeping up on her, Reed, Tom, and George grab her legs and arms and toss her into the pool. They are punished with a thousand lines of Latin repetition and are not allowed to go to the graduation ceremony.

"Henja, dis people dey no dey know what be joke?" I think they wanted to make my brother too serious about the world. "If dey do that I will go for their side and give them a WaWa with ju-ju that will make all the pool green water go away and fill up the pool with dirt so they cannot swim at all."

Caning is a more serious matter. I am lucky, in that I was never caned. There are three canes, depending upon the gravity of the offense. First and least serious is the bamboo cane, which just left red marks across one's bottom. Then there is the knobby cane that left welts and a red mark. Then there is the cane with the lead weight on the end. This left a red mark and a large bruise. Of course, the number of strokes is significant too. The school made sure the punishment doesn't stop at the last stroke of the cane, either. Everybody has to stand in front of the school nurses to take cold baths, so we all could see who had just been caned. The scariest part of the whole process is when the headmaster comes by to say good night, and then says, "Put on your dressing gown and slippers and wait outside my study."

But it is part of the British Empire. I learn about the "police action," that is, the American Revolution. I learn that history is a series of wars that the British won in the end. Peaceful England is always beating the French, Spanish, their colonies, and finally the Germans, Italians, Indians, and so on. Amazing how a small, peaceful democracy can do so much. At the age of ten, I am fascinated how many heroes there are and how many battles there are over trade and their colonies. The English are unabashed in their pride, even in their minor setbacks.

MID-JUNE 1957

When Mr. Tim, our headmaster, takes us into London, he takes us up to Trafalgar Square. It is named after the Battle of Trafalgar in which Admiral Nelson had put a telescope to his blind eye when reading the orders from superiors and then cut the French fleet into two parts and then blew them to bits. Unfortunately, French sharpshooters shot him down in the process. There is a tall black - and- white marble statue of this man in the square, with pigeons everywhere. It is black with age and white from the pigeons dropping donations. Reed and I bring a box of popcorn and hold our arms out for the pigeons to land all around us while we have our picture taken. We are in our best formal coats, but the pigeons are kind — no white donations. But this one-eyed British officer is a hero compared to the one we are to meet in Kaduna some time later. There is nothing like saying that you know the orders, but doing what you thought is needed, winning the battle, but dying a hero. I wonder what they will have done if he had lived? Will he have such big *Ju-Ju* and WaWa?

JUNE 29, 1957

Latin is taught to improve our English—, for some reason I never can understand. We learn Latin to improve our knowledge of the less violent types, like the Romans. *Veni, Vidi, Vici;* Caesar and company. I never get as far as Virgil. In English, essays with details of grammar are pounded in, which will immediately slip back out. Math is more open, and in fact, I move ahead of my American peers. And of course, we learn French.

Discipline is a major factor in the whole operation; even going to the bathroom is checked off to see if we have gone. Mr. Sales did that. Mr. Sales is in a wheelchair; rumor has it he had been in a major battle in World War II. He teaches English with the same firmness that he uses to interrogate us about whether we have gone to the bathroom and then checks us off his list from the head of the stairs. If we say we have not gone, it is off to the matron for a spoonful of cod liver oil. Needless to say, we always say we have gone, since he is at the head of the stairs of the "bogs", as the bathroom is called, and he cannot actually check on us. Constipation from leeks, cabbages, what passed for meat, and milky hot water as tea (high tea is supper) and crumpets is the lesser problem compared to the toilet paper used in the bogs. In America, we are used to soft paper, but this toilet paper is waxed and slippery and in very small pieces.

Then there is a third problem in the bogs. Older boys might gang up on you and hang you upside down, so that Mr. Sales will need to send younger boys back down to the bogs to get you. And then he will box your ears for making his count out of order. All in all, it is wiser to go down the stairs, take the first left to the changing rooms, and wait until Mr. Sales calls your name and number. You then run back up, and find another time to go to the bogs when you can scout out the presence (or hopefully, lack, of older boys), and take your time so you can cope with the toilet paper as well. Still, having your own means to cope with this is an American problem. WaWa.

Twice a day, we go to church. Sometimes in the summer, people faint from the weather, but the service goes on. From what I can tell, after Henry VIII had decided to do away with all but his last wife, they had done away with the confessional and Latin, and that is about it: then they are the Church of England.

The lunch tables are arranged by seniority, and if you don't sit at the head table, you don't get the best pieces. Of course, there is no central heating. The headmaster has a small, coal stove in his office. High tea, consisting of cloudy water and a bun, is supper.

JUNE 30, 1957

I know they are all crazy when they tell me we will have a holiday because the Queen is coming. We all line up on the tarmac. I think she is going to visit. But no, her plane is landing at Gatwick Airport some miles away, and I seriously doubt if she can see us, even if we do wave.

On the positive side, we play a lot of sports every day. Soccer is my favorite, and I make the second team. It is quite an excuse to run all over the place, have a good time, and get exhausted, not to mention some crashing into those who have beat you otherwise. We play that in the fall, and we root for our best team until we are hoarse. In the spring, we run cross-country through the heather bushes and the brush. In the summer, we play cricket. I never make first team, but my American baseball style makes it interesting. In a short bit of time, I can wallop in a few runs before they get me out. I also play silly mid-on or silly mid-off, which are two semi-kamikaze positions between the batsman on both sides, and the bowler next to the other batsman who runs back and forth if the other batsman hit the ball and doesn't get stumped out or have an LBW (leg before wicket). It is confusing for me, so I imagine I am playing shortstop with a great glove, rather than playing with my bare hands. Still, my style of throwing myself at the ground is not seen as British, so I end up watching a lot more matches, and only play on the second-team level.

On Saturdays, we build models and play games. Dan Woods, whose father's farm we later stay at, is reconstructing bone -by -bone a mouse's skeleton from owls' pellets he has collected.

JUNE 31, 1957

My best friend's surname, Blakelock, is easy to remember because he reminds me of my favorite poet, William Blake. The two poems from his *Songs of Experience* I can remember fragments of are "Tiger, tiger, burning bright" and "Pity will be no more, If we did not make somebody Poor: And Mercy no more can be, If all are as happy as we." My particular concern is Blakelock himself. I have to box with him in the school boxing tournament. It is particularly hard because he is my best friend. On top of that, he has five pounds on me and his arms will reach a whole glove longer than my stubby arms. Best friend or not, my national honor is at stake. I am the 'Yank,' after all. Besides, I have the number 67 at school, and Reed has the number 68, so we fight regularly in the locker room because we are on top of each other. I mean, as regularly as brothers may. If anyone tries to break us up, we beat them up and then go back to our own family fight. So, I think I have a secret weapon (or training anyway). On the day of the fight, it is boxing gloves and the rules of Queensbury, so I cannot hit below his short pant belt. By then, he has seen Reed and I battle, so he has his pants high and part of his lower hips covered, just where I used to pound Reed, to win my share of brotherly love. I have practiced my left jab and my right hook, and I am scared, but angrier that I have to battle my best friend. I figure if I can win against my younger brother's temper and love for me, the Englishman friend is doomed to my persistence. Besides, my final weapon has been that Reed always told other kids, larger and smaller, who did him in, that I will do them in. When they surprise me by their attacks, I have my brother's love and experience fighting with him that allows me to defeat those bigger than Blakelock. So I have this experience too.

When the match begins, the whole school is present. Blakelock circles like a cat on the outside. I take over the center of the ring to challenge him to do battle. Because his reach is longer than mine, I have to expend two or three jabs and a right to get close to him. But he will dance away. I keep chasing him for the first four rounds. By round five, I have not gotten inside his defense to score more than a few points. At that point, Blakelock begins to rain blows on me. The crowd begins to yell, "Blakelock! Blakelock!" and "Come on, Yank!" They do not care who wins, just as long as somebody gets flattened. Twice, I manage to get inside his reach and pound his ribs. But each time, the referee breaks us up since Blakelock's pants are so high. The crowd boos. It is me they are disappointed with. I think, *"Never you mind. They haven't watched enough cowboy movies."* Besides, I can find no better way to get inside his reach. The pounding from Blakelock gets worse. He even manages to get my nose to bleed a bit. I refuse to quit. The crowd begins to scream, "Stay in there, Yank!."

I take everything he dishes out, and I defend myself well. I can find no way to get past his longer arms; the last part of the match is his. I am bloodied. I lose. But I am still standing at the end of the fight. My friendship with Blakelock cools a bit at this point, since I think he hasn't made it clear he will not battle a friend. But I am an American, not as much into duty and school pride as he is. The next year, in Switzerland, a pair of 180-pound American twins teaches me the uppercut, the American boxing move that makes longer arms no question, as the British just don't teach it. WaWa for Yanks and the uppercuts, but where is the Ju-Ju when you need it?

JULY 5, 1957

The most fun is after the lights are out. Dorms will raid each other. If you decide you are to raid, you stuff one long sock in with its mate and put your slippers in your belt like knives to throw, and you take your toothbrush cup to hit the recalcitrant ones over the head. The trick of the matter is to sneak in without waking anybody and turn over all the beds at once. The trouble is, if they hear you coming, they can rise up out of their beds and trap you in the back of the dorm. So the lightest sleepers sleep in the front part of the dorm. I get the privilege of being able to sleep in the front of the dorm.

One morning at about 2:30 a.m., I hear some whispering up the walk. I wake up the other members of the dorm. First we put on our belts, and then we put our slippers into our belts. We quickly stuff the other sock into our large socks to make sock truncheons, and then lay back down to sleep, with one hand underneath our pillows. In addition, quietly and quickly, we move our older boys to the beds in the middle of the dorm and put our younger and faster boys in the back of the dorm. Sure enough, it is Dorm Six pulling a raid on us. They creep down the middle of the dorm to attack us and turn over our beds. As soon as they reach the other end of the dorm by the window, we rise up as one and begin to attack them with pillows, slippers, and sock a truncheons. The place is a whirling dervish of flying objects and the warning cry of, "They're on to us; run before we're caught!"

In a move that would have made Admiral Nelson of the Battle of Trafalgar proud, we cut off the invading marauders in the middle of the group, by overturning two beds in the middle of the room ourselves, and concentrating our attack on a trapped group at the end of the dorm. We can hear the voice of one of the matrons, yelling, "Who is causing all this noise? I will report them to the headmaster!" The trapped groups of four, or five, begin to get desperate and throw the metal mugs in which we keep our toothbrushes and toothpaste in, off the windowsills onto the side we control, between them and the door, like grenades. One boy, Eric, dives over the beds and escapes. The others cannot get past the wall of pillows, beds, sock-a-truncheons and flying slippers.

Sure enough, the matrons switch on the lights, and there in the chaos are four number- six dormers who do not belong to our dorm, and have no escape. Six candidates are held responsible for those fatal words from the headmaster when he came around at night after lights- out with a flashlight. "Smith, Jr., put on your slippers and robe and wait outside my study."

The following morning, we see two brown- bruised fannies and four red-striped ones as we take our cold baths.

JULY 8, 1957

Guzz (candy) treats are another late-night, early-morning pleasure. Since I can wake myself up by the chimes of the chapel clock, I am always picked to get us up. Most dorms have secret floorboards, but ours do not, so we have to hide all our candy, biscuits, and sardines someplace else. So we choose underneath the altar in the chapel, figuring no one will look there. Sure enough, we are right, and no one ever found our stash. It is a little funny to be praying to our food, but it did a lot to dispel my notion that God is in the corner over the altar.

Every year, the chestnut trees ripen, and the chestnuts fall to the ground. Juniors and seniors use penknives to cut round holes in the chestnuts, put a string through a hole in the nut, and tie a knot at one end bigger than the hole. Then the conkers contest begins. The contest is to smash your opponent's chestnut into pieces, so it will fall off the string. The best shots are those that come with a downward motion of the arm, with the maximum length of the string with its conker hitting right onto the hole where the cover, the inside soft part of the chestnut, and the string all come together. This properly cracks the case or the whole chestnut into pieces. But the *ju-ju* of the masters (teachers) is always better than the students. They will destroy all newcomers until there are only master conkers left over. Then the real championship begins. For the first two years I was there, Mr. Weeks, the math teacher, always won. Even in the following three years, when Reed is there, Mr. Weeks is the proper number-one man in conkers. Reed wrote to me, wondering if the secret of Mr. Weeks's victories is that he has crops of chestnuts from the previous years dried to the point that they broke or smashed the next year's crop.

AUGUST 9, 1957

Reed and I spend three vacations in Great Britain, and go on one outing with our headmaster. Our dad decides we ought to have watches, so the headmaster, Mr. Tim, takes us out to a number of jewelers until we find watches we like. He even buys us ice cream. I think he is pleased that Mr. Shoesmith, a British friend of my parents and a former member of the Cold Stream Guard, has come to visit us boys. Hence by association, we are obviously all right. After all, we are the first Americans to have gone to Copthorne School, and we are not in the habit of letting it be known that my parents rent the Jaguar and chauffeur on their visits. That would have created the impression that we are not as well off as some of the other students.

The first vacation in Great Britain is to Mr. Woods's farm, when Dad, Mom, and Coagie are living in Abba, Nigeria. Mr. Woods thinks we should learn another sport and see more of London. We see Buckingham Palace and go to a number of museums, most of which have pictures of serious- looking people sitting on horses or standing next to dogs or "significant others," as we say today. What makes an impression on me is the stairwell up to see the Queen's jewels. The stairwell is narrow, made of stone, and goes round and round; it is the Tower of London.

I think about Queen Elizabeth I. What a queen she'd been! Just like her father, King Henry VIII, she'd put relatives to the axe. Her own half-sister, Queen Mary of Scotland, a woman who the textbooks say had ice for blood. A woman who, when she knew she was going to be beheaded, practiced for a week to get her head and neck just in the right place for the executioner. Then, on the fateful day, the executioner is nervous and he only hit her neck partially, so with blood streaming down from her neck, Mary Ann Boleyn, Queen of Scotland, moved her head and neck back into the correct spot for the headsman to finish the job. I mean to say, a bit much, eh, what?

SEPTEMBER 8, 1957

I am going to talk about horses. Well, Mr. Woods is not a yeoman farmer for no reason. His family went back many generations in the cemetery next to the small village chapel, where his youngest brother is a minister. He is landed gentry, and he knows no education is complete without knowing how to ride horseback. Mr. Woods also has thousands of chickens. There are so many chickens that many of them roosts in the trees. Every night, Mr. Woods takes his shotgun and goes around to check the chicken house. At first, I think he is worried about the fox getting into the chicken house. No, he explains, it is the chickens in the trees he is worried about. A smart fox shows up and walks slowly around the tree. The chickens watch every move. Then, when he has their attention, he runs around and around the tree until one of the chickens gets dizzy and falls out. My respect for foxes grows quite a lot upon hearing this. WaWa foxes.

OCTOBER 9, 1957

Reed and I are too young for polo, but not for the possibility that our future dates might want to go horseback riding or fox hunting. Mr. Woods has that in mind. Reed and I, on the other hand, are still young enough to think we might move out west and work as cowboys, roping steers. Mr. Woods sends us to riding school in the next village. Given that we are Americans, our instructors make much of the fact that there are two ways to ride: the British way and the American way. The American way, we are told, is not for the civilized. In England, as the horse trots you pumped up and down as the horse goes along, and you do that a bit faster at a canter and finally, at top speed, the same as you gallop.

All of this is fine in theory, until Reed and I are put on horses. The horses are going down cobblestone streets for a slow ride. They place my horse in the rear of the formation of five students and the instructor. My horse takes exception to this placement by putting its ears down, taking off like a rocket, and taking a good bite out of every horse it passes. As soon as it takes a bite out of my brother's, which is in front of me, that horse takes off after mine in revenge, and so on down the line. Reed and I fly down the streets, sparks flying off the cobbles. Horses are neighing, and all six horses are cantering and galloping down the streets. The instructor has no control over the situation. As it turns out, my horse is simply not English in style, nor will it allow itself to be last on the block, civilized or not. WaWa horses.

DECEMBER 24.–25, 1957

We are taken from London to a Welsh farm for our second vacation in England. The *Aerosmith's* are glider fanatics; so one Saturday they take us to an airfield. Reed and I are each given a separate ride in a glider. A small single-engine plane pulls the gliders aloft. The plane pulls the glider silently up into the air. At two thousand feet, the pilot of the glider pushes a handle and we are free of our tow. He turns to the right, and the horizon slides around slowly. It is so silent, we can barely hear the wind, and the glider feels like a ping-pong ball on a saltwater pond. The pilot shifts us in another direction to look for updrafts to ride on, but we have no luck that day. The glider circles three times more, but still has to land at its original point of departure.

Reed goes up for his ride, but fares no better. But the Aerosmith's, as I think of them then, think Reed and I still need a "spot of adventure," as they put it. So they ask, "Have either of you ever been over?"

"No," Reed and I reply in unison, but we are too polite to ask what that means. Besides, the glider flight has enamored us temporarily with the idea we can behave like birds with no fear of flying at all. So they strap us in together in the rumble seat in the tow plane and send us back into the sky. This time, the noise is horrific, and everything vibrates and shakes as though it will fall apart at any time. As the plane flies up, everything is fine. Then the plane dives straight down, and my stomach goes twice the distance to the ground. After what seems like crash time, the pilot pulls the plane up, and I begin to feel a huge weight all over. Gradually, the whole horizon begins to vanish, and as it does, I can see the sky. Then the dirt from the floor of the plane begins to float up towards the top of the cockpit. The dirt floats back down as we complete our loop. No doubt, this is the first time I see dirt rise up and vanish, too. *Too bad I can't do that regularly without a bath, I thought.* Still, my stomach seems less enthusiastic about this "going over" business.

When we write the 'rents about this, we get no response. It is as though it never happened. When Reed and I get down to

Kaduna, Nigeria, Mom says, "No more gliding, not now, never." Reed and I are perplexed. Later, we find out that two of Dad and Mom's friends have been killed in a gliding accident in Accra, the same week our cheery letters had arrived.

The second part of this vacation is to a dairy farm in Wales. There I learn to milk a cow by hand, and how farmers keep their hands warm by pressing them between the udder and leg of the cow. This keeps their hands from chapping, even though machines milk the cows. But the best part is to go to the highest hills and look over and see the green Isle of Ireland. I used to spend hours wondering what the land of my ancestors is really like. The other part is my discovery of an oil-soaked guillemot bird. Every day I feed him and brush his oiled feathers, gently washing them with soapy detergent and water. When I get back to London, I visit the RSPCA (Royal Society for the Prevention of Cruelty to Animals). There I receive a lecture on how I should have left the bird alone. I am furious. Instead of being helpful, I get a useless lecture. *Very British, I thought.* Of course, the bird did die later, but with some help, I feel it could have made it. WaWa.

SIERRA LEONE, WEST AFRICA

DECEMBER 1958

When you're having fun, time flies. Reed and I fly to Dakar, in French West Africa. The flight is so bumpy that champagne is foaming onto the carpets. Air Chance, as I call Air France, even lets an unopened bottle of champagne go by, so I slip it into my flight bag to give to my parents. At Dakar, Reed and I let the younger kids play with the lizards, since we are old hands at that.

A DC-3, like in the old-time movies, is wheeled out, and all of us are packed in like sardines in a can. It is a short, bumpy flight. My parents take pictures, and it is hard to tell what is shaking more, the plane or my mother's hands on the movie camera. After landing, we take a fifteen-minute ride, which is very choppy over the murky water. But all is clear and calm by the time we arrive in the port of Sierra Leone.

Our new house is up on a hill, and built on concrete supports so it will not get washed away in the rainy season. A word about rainy seasons: in some places, it rains every day at the same time; others, a black line appears in the sky, and then it rains hard. In other places, it rains hard all the time. But in those areas where it rains hard and suddenly, concrete channels have to be built because people get washed into the ocean and drown. Frankly, that too is not enough, because from time to time, people fall into the concrete channels. Since they are used to walking along their sides or in the channels, but then not before a rush of water sweeps them away. People know about this, but then ...WaWa!

Freetown is built on a hill, so that makes a difference; because the house is partly on concrete stilts on the back side and parts of the front with room for the water to go through down the hill. We have a small back garden. Reed and I only spend a month here, so Dad gets the Land Rover, and we load up with spear guns, masks, and flippers and head off to find an empty cove. The coves are coral blue, except when run-off rainwater turns them a dirty gray, or the clouds turn them a plain, clean gray. Our stay is more often than not blessed with sunshine and aqua- blue coves, in all sizes.

The Land Rover is often the vehicle you will see on safaris in East Africa. It's a big, square metal box, with windows in all four directions and a roof with a shiny metal bar all the way around, so that extra goods can be strapped on top. It has a look that says, "Come over, come over. I will run you over." I think you do not measure its engines in horsepower, but more like tank power, except it rides higher than a tank. So, deep-rutted sandy roads that turn to coral or rock are nothing, nor are trails with bush protruding to dare us to stop. WaWa to the Land Rover.

Anyway, with a four-wheel-drive Land Rover, we can pick and choose among the many unspoiled coves available. With a nice picnic lunch, it is an all-day affair. Reed and I have been taught to swim by the British, and we take our masks and spear guns in search of prey. Usually we get nothing, but it is a pleasure to see the coral and small fish. My father, who goes farther out, says he is cruising around following a large grouper, when the shadow of something bigger than him passes above him; and from then on, he stays a bit closer in.

One day when the water is a bit murky and the top of Coagie"s tube is blown out, Reed saves Coagie's life. We have a party to celebrate Reed rescuing Coagie. Coagie insists he wants to find out what will happen if he pulls out the top of the tube and then drinks much of the Gulf of Guinea. WaWa.

DECEMBER 15, 1958

Coagie likes to test things to see how they work out. Coagie has a friend who is related to Sorry, the cook — a *picken* whose name is Tom. Tom convinces Coagie that green peppers on the wild bush have even more *ju-ju* power than the red ones do, or even the yellow ones, for that matter. So Coagie decides he wants to see just how much *ju-ju* power a small green pepper has from a wild bush. So he collects two small green peppers from the bush growing outside the compound. *"Hmm,"* he thinks to himself, *"who should I test it on?" "Mom will be great, " he thought, "because her energy level has been low from entertaining all those visiting businessmen from New York."*

He goes in search for Mom, and when he finds her, he says, "Mom, this will fix you up right away. Tom told me it have extra *ju-ju* to fix anything."

Mom is used to seeing red or yellow peppers, as well as the hot ones, but she has no idea about the smaller green ones. They look just like regular green peppers that have no heat.

"Thank you, Coagie. That's very thoughtful," Mom says.

Mom puts the small green pepper in her mouth and bites into it. It has *ju-ju,* no doubt. As the heat spreads into Mom's mouth, she screams and jumps up to chase Coagie. Coagie, sensing his experiment has mixed results, runs for the door. He only beats Mom to the door because she needs to turn back to find something to drink, to cool the furnace burning in her mouth. Coagie runs all the way to find Tom. "Tom, Tom,!" he yells. "But why dis ting? I give my mother, and she be plenty mad. This be no ju-ju. This be bad ju-ju."

Tom comes out and says, "I say this pepper be big ju-ju. I no did tell you can eat it all together to get the ju-ju power. You can only use a small part to put in the food to give another person proper, number- one- type ju-ju."

Coagie says, "I dey go, come now. My mother thinks I be fla-fla boy."

Tom laughs, "Yes, this be true now. Maybe you can fix it. I will not come your side until you come again my side and get me, since your Madame, she be plenty angry with you."

Coagie goes and hides in the help's quarters until Dad comes home for lunch. He runs out into the driveway and tells Dad that, really, he had only wanted to help Mom by this *Ju-Ju*. Dad goes in to talk with Mom. They decide that the 'rents are not suitable for medical experiments or experiments of any kind. Coagie is grounded for three weeks. He gets no allowance, and he does not get to visit Tom for that period of time. Truly, small green peppers, or red ones, or yellow ones, are powerful *Ju-Ju*. But there will always be a WaWa if you don't know who to try it on, or how.

When we are not snorkeling, my father takes us down to the docks to fish. We never catch anything, even though we can see the fish. So the driver who comes to pick us up buys some local fish for us so we can return home triumphant. But that is not to say the local kids do not do well. They bait huge hooks with fish and throw them way out in the water, and tie themselves to the line. Then they sit around and talk. Suddenly, one of them flies out into the ocean, and everybody else has to jump in to save him. At the other end there may be a sixty or seventy-pound grouper, almost as big as the boy. It does not happen every day, but it is exciting when it does. WaWa.

DECEMBER 20, 1958

Dad's penchant for farming experiments persists. He sends away for scientifically tested beans spaced evenly on plastic strips, so we can have fresh beans. The gardener, who speaks only Creole, not Pidgin English, says to him, "Dese beans dey not dey grow here."

"Never you mind," my father says, "plant them." And the gardener does. Then, after the bean sprouts appear, my father goes to him and says, "Cut down sticks to match each one."

The gardener says, "But why do dis foolish ting?" But he does it. When the termites hear about the American pole beans, they come in and eat them all. But the twigs grow nicely each equidistant from one another, and my father never has the heart to cut them down. But we never have beans. WaWa.

Mom has a talent for being a good listener. Wherever she goes, people have some instinct to tell her their life stories. In the States, she comes back from shopping and later talk about the butcher, the baker, the checkout counter person, etc. Soon they are her regular friends, and when she hears a particularly difficult story, she says, "That poor old soul." And if they have been wronged, she says, "Heavens to Murgatroyid." Dad calls it Mom's "poor old soul theory."

I'm not sure where Murgatroiyd is. I think it is an angel's commuter stop, somewhere between Earth and heaven. But I have no idea if angels go there to work or to vacation. Given the way Mom says it, it seems unimportant to ask, since it seems like an OK place.

Dad is not immune to the "poor old soul theory" himself. Both of them sometimes end up supporting a "poor old soul" for different reasons in Sierra Leone. The cook, Sorry, who Dad says made him feel sorry, has a fourteen-year-old wife, and her cousin introduced Mom to an African whose Christian name is Henry. "Dis man," he tells Mom, "want to go to school to better himself. So, he dey know dey not have money for dis ting. Please, Madame, can you see your way to your heart to help him get an education?" Mother says she will see what she can do, but she wants to talk with Dad. Henry comes to the house every other day for the next week. At the end of the week, he says to Mom, "Madame, I de beg you, dis ting be everyting; I need for dey money, it no be that much." Mom has been talking the matter over with Dad, and it is true that Dad feels that if his farming experiments have not worked, an educated African will be able to out-smart this WaWa problem, at least. So Dad and Mom decide to send Henry to school. Henry says that the school is up-country, and he will send the bills to Dad and Mom for tuition, books, and living allowance.

Henry keeps sending letters requesting more money for uniforms. So, after a while, Dad goes to visit him. In the village of the return address from the bills, he finds Henry living in a large village house with his two wives and six children. So, Dad asks Henry what is going on and what is he learning? Henry says, "I am learning how to live comfortably in this African village, master." WaWa.

DECEMBER 26, 1958

Boxing Day in Sierra Leone is quite a holiday for both Africans and Europeans. The European Department of Public Workmen, or the D.P.W. men, as my father calls them, takes Reed, Dad, and me to an African celebration. The Europeans stand in one part of an oblong area, and the Africans fill the rest on the other side. The drumming fills the area like torrential rains. A tall African signals for silence. Then, a number of Africans bring forth the cardboard boxes of empty brown beer bottles. The bottles are brought to the center of the area. Then you can see and hear them being smashed into pieces on the ground. With another signal, the drumming fills the air again. A circle of male dancers begin to dance around the brown glass pieces. Then with a third signal, they dance right onto the glass. There they dance several small circles on the glass, with cheers from Africans and the Public Works people looking on. After ten minutes, the music stops and the dancers bring themselves to the Europeans and show them their feet, to prove they are unharmed, since everyone knows Europeans only believe in ju-ju if they can see it. Sure enough, Reed, Dad, and I can see that their feet are fine. But maybe, I think, Africans walk barefoot if they are poor, so their feet are callused and can handle broken glass.

They must have anticipated that we will not believe the power of the ju-ju, because they sweep away the brown glass and move us to a new position, where we gather around a small, shallow ditch stretching some ten or twenty feet, about ten inches deep and about twelve inches wide. There, a circle of dancers brings forth small charcoal braziers with red coals, with the English still looking on. Reed and I are a bit nervous about this one. The ditch is definitely too deep not to burn the feet of the African dancers. All we can do is wait and see. The drumming begins again, more like a throb of excitement. This time, the coals are systematically layered in the ditch for all to see.

When the dancers appear, the crowd of Africans let out a sigh of terror and appreciation, and the dancers begin to circle around the ditch. This time, the sweat flies off their bodies as they dance and fly into the crowd their eyes begin to roll up and down so that you can see the whites of their eyes. The head dancer takes the lead and, dances onto the coals. The African crowd begins to moan the appropriate words of their tribe's magic ju-ju. Everybody continues to dance on through the ditch at least once and, then stop, sweating and breathing heavily until their skin is glassy. The British have remained motionless and silent. Reed and I line up in the queue to see the African dancers' feet. The Africans did have to brush away some coal dust off the bottoms of their feet. Apart from that, their feet looked fine! WaWa.

Reed and I are quite impressed. Dad says they are using hypnosis. Then the drumming starts up again, and the dancers appear on wooden stilts so you can see them above the crowd. The crowd claps to their movements on the stilts. By now, Reed and I want to go home, because we are tired, so Dad takes us. I watch the stilted dancers out of the back window of the car, and I wonder what hypnosis is, but I am too thirsty to think about it for long.

DECEMBER 31, 1958

At the New Year's party, my father's company buys cases of champagne and caviar, and the British governor comes. He does not leave, and it is quite the scandal, because the other embassy parties that he didn't go to, felt he violated protocol. Reed and I help polish off some champagne ourselves; it tastes like ginger ale, but we both need naps before the afternoon is over.

But four weeks is not so very long, and soon we are on the launch back to the DC-3. At least this time, I get to sit next to Reed on the way back, again on Air Chance. I pick on Air France because the ride between London and Paris is bumpy; nevertheless, their pheasant under glass is excellent.

Some years later, I found out that an additional incident occurred between Dad's company and the union. Ghana had a 15 percent higher literacy rate than the State of Maine, and so did many other West African countries like Sierra Leone, because most children went to school of some sort or another. Alassa and Alakeleen were literate in Arabic, from going to a religious school.

The Ashanti-hene was said to educate one son in the African tradition for each sent abroad for schooling. The latter were known as "been- to's" (gone abroad). WaWa.

My father later told me a company story in Sierra Leone. A labor strike erupted, as the union wanted to add a third man to the petrol lorry. (There is a driver and a driver's mate, but sometimes the truck has to decant small amounts of gasoline, and they wanted someone to do that.) During the negotiations, the company says over and over again that one man can do the whole job. Mean while, the union negotiators are certain they are against redundancy too. Hence, they put up placards saying, "Redundancy must go." In the end, the company settles for a driver and a driver's mate.

Dad, Mom, Coagie and Café au Lait, the dog, are transferred from Sierra Leone to Liberia. As they leave Freetown early in the morning, the sun is rising and the rays goes through the eastern windows of the airport building, right in to the customs area. Mom is carrying a jewelry box with some rhinestone necklaces and bracelets. The jewelry box is lined with black velvet. When Mom opens it to show the customs man, the rays of the sun bounces all over, and the rhinestones look like diamonds. "Ahh… ha!" says the customs man, "You are smuggling diamonds!"

Mom pulls herself even more erectly and says in an imperious tone, "If these are diamonds, I will would not be standing here at this ungodly hour discussing my jewelry."

With a second's hesitation, the customs officer says, "So right. On you go, Madame." WaWa, Mom.

MONROVIA, LIBERIA

There is always a place to go that turns out to be different than you think. Roberts Field in Monrovia is hot, muggy, and slow. The Customs men are semi-surly and oppressive. Our house is right on the Monrovian River, so it is tropical in the sense of Bogart in the *African Queen*.

In a similar manner, Mother does not like Monrovia. She spends a lot of time staring at this big dead tree in one corner of the compound. She has other minor problems. Every time she buys crayfish that look like lobsters the tentacles disappear. It turns out Liberians believe that the tentacles can be ground up and put in your food as poison. So someone will steal them to prevent that from happening to them.

Coagie also has a mixed time in Monrovia. He is stung badly by a Portuguese man-o-war (a jellyfish), but my parents take care of it medically. The beach where Coagie got stung is a favorite of Reed's and mine during our stay in Liberia. The surf is quite choppy there. As a result, the water always has a sandy, and gritty character to it. Reed and I are better swimmers because of practice in the green, and murky waters in the school pool back in England. That is, we can dog paddle quite well, even venturing into the water over our heads. After Coagie's experience with the man-o-war, we keep a careful lookout for them.

Something else has struck me about Coagie's experience with the man-o-war. I remember the treatments Coagie had to go through for his birthmark on his thigh back in the States. Every two weeks, we had to go from Baimville to Newburgh, New York, for Coagie's treatments. There in the hospital that looked like a concrete version of the Neuia Amsterdam, Coagie had to have dry ice put on his birthmark because, they said, when he grows up, it might get cut, and he can die from the bleeding. Then Dad took us all to downtown Newburgh for ice cream. Newburgh is on a steep hill across the Hudson River from the town of Beacon. The ice cream shop was at the top of the hill. After ice cream, Dad drove down the main street at top speed, as though we are going to drive right into the river. It felt as if your stomach was on a roller coaster. We screamed and begged Dad not to drive us into the river. He always slowed down at the bottom, and we go home and forget the incident until the next treatment. Coagie does not; he cries whenever he sees the hospital, so I know they are torturing my brother, whatever they say, and I hate them for that.

Now what worries me, in this case, is what I told Reed: "What if the Portuguese man-o-war wrapped around you and left scars like those on Coagie? Will they have to torture you, because if you got cut when you are a grown-up, it will bleed so much you can die?" Reed gets so scared, he tells Dad what I said. Dad tells me they did not use dry ice to cure man-o-war stings. I still think scars and tortures are to stop bleeding! It is okay to get the attention by swallowing a two-shilling piece and having it removed in Accra, but this? Man-o-war is bad *ju-ju*.

Mom and Dad decide to hire Sammy to be Coagie's playmate. The two of them play crazy eights, stuffing half the deck into the couch to cheat. That's probably why my brother Coagie is a lawyer today and is working to enforce the Bar of Ohio's ethics .

When Reed and I arrive in Monrovia, we think Sammy has been hired only because Dad and Mom thought Coagie needed someone to play crazy eights with and to prevent Coagie from falling into the Monrovian River that goes right past one side of our compound, where there is no fence. Originally, Sammy moved into the compound for two reasons. Sammy had been living in a small fishing village two miles up the river from us. He got sick, and the witch doctor went to examine him. The witch doctor knew what Sammy had, so he went and applied the tribal rule: banishment from his parents, the village, and the tribe. Sammy is put on the road to die, to save the village. Sammy tells his story to Ipsom, our first steward, and begs that Madame should get the white doctor. Ipsom tells Mom that it is true, for certain diseases, a village puts a person out to prevent the others from getting the disease.

Mom is not ready to simply have the boy move in, so she sends for the doctor to find out what Sammy has. Sure enough, he has a serious disease that is quite contagious: smallpox! Everyone in the house has to be re-inoculated, and Sammy moves into the small back room in the help's quarters, underneath the main house. Sammy recovers, and when Coagie discovers a partner who cheats at crazy eights by stuffing cards down into the couch as well as he does, the 'rents think, "So be it." And that is how we find Sammy and Coagie playing cards when we arrived, and still playing cards when we leave. WaWa to Mom's "poor old soul" theory.

APRIL 6, 1959

Reed and I know a vacation when we see one, so we get involved in fishing. There is a concrete bridge about 150 feet above the river, and we use meat for bait. But that doesn't work, so we use baby birds, as our African adviser told us to; that doesn't seem to work either. Then one day, I discover why. The Africans who come by in canoes are checking our lines and taking anything we have caught. So instead we collect nests of baby birds to bring up, and give them to Mother to take care of after we leave. Long after we are gone, all but one flew away.

APRIL 17--19, 1959

Two other exciting things happened in Monrovia. One is that the yardman, John, saves us from a green spitting mamba; he just cuts off its head with a sharp machete. The other is that my mother saves a man from drowning. She is walking along the river when she sees a wooden canoe tipped over. One man scrambles to the shore, saying he can't swim, but neither can the other man. My mother orders the man on the bank back into the water to save the one in the river, which he does. If you have known my mother, you will know that her orders are obeyed. The state of Liberia gave her an award for her effort.

Yacetti, or *Yacettio,* is an excellent pidgin word to know; it means finished, over, gone forever, vanished, terminated, etc. Coagie gets to be quite an expert with *yacetti* for two reasons. He stuffed cards in the couch on which he and Sammy sat and played crazy eights, and he will yell out *"yacetti"* to his own game. In addition, Coagie will be eating *fou-fou* at the table, and he will sing out *"yacetti"* for extra emphasis, so that Sammy, Reed, and I will watch as he gets seconds to continue on eating his *fou-fou.*; as we watch, the orange ring will grow around his lips, and his lips began to swell.

APRIL 25, 1959

Yacetti is also an optimistic word; it means finished when it comes to the heat waves of Liberia. Those smothering wet blankets of muggy heat and humidity means that sweat can't leave your body because there is more heat outside your body than in the air. *Yacetti* to this, *yacetti* to that. The insides of the bedrooms are another place where it is possible for a *yacetti* to happen in relationship to the heat waves and the high humidity. Since the bedrooms have air conditioning, we used to sing together, "*Yacetti, yacetti,*" when Dad and Mom say it is time to go to bed, because we will be relieved from the heat.

Dad and Mom do not always tell Coagie when there is trouble, that is, at least not in the case of the Monrovia River and what happened there. The boat we have is really a large wooden rowboat with an outboard motor at the back, and some oars to row in case the engine fails. Dad, Mom, and Coagie went go down to the river for a late-afternoon ride. Everything is going smoothly. It is only a couple of miles until the river empties into the ocean. There it gets full currents and waves from the sandbars the murky river deposits as it enters the cleaner Gulf of Guinea. Dad is planning to turn the boat around and return up the river. They reach a safe distance from the sandbars and begin to turn. The propeller bites into something it cannot spit out, and the engine slows to a crawl, even at top speed. Dad does not initially worry, because they are still making progress back up the river. But the tide turns, and the river basin begins to empty faster and faster into the ocean; now they are making no progress at all.

Dad switches seats with Mom and begins to row as well. Mid-afternoon is turning to early evening, and in Equatorial Africa there is little twilight and no Daylight Savings. Coagie thinks Dad is showing off and tells him, "Dad, stop showing off." He

ACCRA REVISITED

Accra Airport is its usual pleasant self when Reed and I arrive. Our new split-level house in Tesano is more modern, and its compound is not so large. Still, there is room enough for a monkey and a turkey.

As the Gold Coast becomes Ghana, two things happen. I grow a bit taller and heavier than Reed. It is not more than an inch, but it is noticeable, so I stop worrying that I will be mistaken for Reed's twin. If Ghanaians do not look at us as equals before, they do now with national independence. That is good, I think; some people want us to leave Ghana also, and I know my father's company is preparing to have all Ghanaian staff run Mobil's retail operations.

As I only go either where my family sends me or where they take me, I pay less attention to what is going on with the company and more with my usual friends. Well, Reed and I are walking along the path to the village, and we pass the big tree and cross the road that goes to Kumasi. A tall, heavy, African teenager jumps out of the bush and begins to beat me. He offers no reason but the prospect of a savage beating. I am bigger and heavier than I used tells Dad several times that he is showing off, as Dad continues to row the heavy wooden boat up the river.

They make it back, just as the sun sinks and the sky goes from gray to black and the stars pop out of the heavens. I find out about this in bits and pieces from Mom's correspondence, which she sends us because school forces us to write to our parents every Saturday, under strict supervision. When I ask Dad in Liberia, he says if Coagie hadn't said what he did, Dad might not have had the energy to row that soggy wooden boat to safety. After that, Dad always chose to go up river for our adventures and outings in Monrovia. WaWa, Coagie.

APRIL 30, 1959

Dad's green boat is just big enough for the five of us, so we occasionally tour the river or fish. One time, I get a heavy line and attached a huge wooden plug with large hooks on it. We are going up the river nicely, but start to slow down. My father pulls on the line and tells me we probably have a log on the end of it. So we circle back. My mother pulls on the line and jerks it back. Now we know we have a fish almost as big as the boat we are in. So my father guns the motor in an attempt to drown it. Finally, in a sandy part of the river, we beach the boat, and my father gets out the movie camera. The fish is still alive, so my father hits it over the head, and an eye pops out. Of course, in the movie of this event, we show only the other side. The fish is a four-and-a-half-foot barracuda. The trouble is, nobody can eat the fish after what my father has done, and we have to give it away to the help.

to be, yet I cannot go anywhere. He has me on the ground with his first three blows. I yell to Reed, who is behind me, to run, but Reed becomes furious. "How dare you beat my brother?" he yells, and rips a young tree out of the ground to pound the African over his head, raining blow after blow. Faced with this new, possibly crazier attacker, the African runs back into the bush. Trembling and shaking but thankful for my brother's courage and loyalty, I go with Reed to see Alassa.

Alassa knows which person it is when we described his size and what he had done. "Dis boy, he dey say to everyone, white man no dey have any ju-ju *ju-ju* anymore and dey all no good anyway." Whether the last point is true or not, Reed still has *ju-ju*. WaWa, Reed.

Alassa and Alakaleen are still in the area, so we hang out with them. Alassa tells me he is studying witchcraft, which makes sense to me. He shows me his collection of small birds with sticks pointing in different directions that he put over the round wood and mud door of his father's house as examples of his new craft. I take it for granted that this is the way you go about these matters. When Alassa and I have been in the bush together, he has been able to spot when an animal had just been nearby or had made a tunnel. So, it works very well for him.

When I try to get a rifle to shoot the wild bush cows that Alassa tells me are occasionally around, I have no luck with my parents. They only support my ambitions of being a great hunter, armed with a slingshot assisted by ju-ju

JULY 5, 1959

Alakaleen and Reed used to go off to the empty construction sites near the area of our Tesano compounds. There they used to smoke so many cigarettes, their heads would spin, and they turned gray in Alakaleen's case and green in Reed's case. Rather than buying cigarettes, I save my money to spend on more expensive items: red rubber slingshots. However, at some point in one of these smoking parties, Alakaleen and Reed got into a fight. So, for a while, only Alassa and I are friends. Before Reed and I go back to school in England, he and Alakaleen become friends again. In part, this has to do with the red putt-putt, which is the red American bicycle that had been mine. I had given it to Reed since I had outgrown it in Accra.

We had brought it back to Africa from Baimville, New York, where we had returned for six months. I think its heyday had been in Kumasi, speeding around with Monkmonk perched on my shoulder. I have not wanted to give it up, but in the Luago Gate, my Uncle Peter had given me a large Raleigh bicycle with gears that he had gotten in Cambridge, England, where he crewed against the Oxford team of Oarsman. So, I waited until I grew into that larger bicycle at the second Accra visit, and the red putt-putt became Reed's. The handlebar of the putt-putt broke one day when Reed was speeding very fast around a corner. So Reed gave it to Alakaleen, who repaired it by putting a stick in the bar. Some form of the red putt-putt, or of its parts, is probably still going around that Tesano village today. Good ole' putt-putt. What a machine!

JULY 9, 1959

By the second tour in Accra, Alassa, Reed, Alakaleen, and I get permission to take the mammy wagons to the market, but Alakaleen and Alassa in particular, think we should take a bus. It is less crowded, and we might get seats for a trip, which is twice as long as by car. So "Jesus saves" goes by with its goats and chickens, and "Nobody knows but Jesus" goes by with people up on the roof. Finally, the bus comes, but it is loaded with people.

"Never you mind," says Alakaleen. "Dis people no dey go far."
Sure enough, at the next stop, a lot of people get off. "It be two
o'clock…dis people dey going home-self for nap…Fine, fine."

Reed and I are certainly the first white people, in a while,
to use the bus; everyone looks us over with great curiosity.
The busy chatter of men and women with chickens, plantains,
groundnuts, yams, cassavas, and other fruits and vegetables
in white enameled pans comes to a halt. The more everybody
examines us, the more Alakaleen swells with pride. He says
in a loud voice, "What be dis ting? You know dey never see
white people before. Dis be my friends, you be from 'bush' side
and fla-fla boys." The bus breaks up with laughter, and regular
conversation resumes.

The bus smells like the yellow soap and talcum powder of the
women and bittersweet shaving lotion of a few men traveling on
business to the city in their best clothes, or in one case a western
suit. Other than the worn-out spring of the seats and the fact that
the bus roof is so loaded that it leans to one side, it is just another
bus going somewhere on the road. Reed and I relax to enjoy the
trip. Alassa begins to discuss what he looks for in the red rubber
bicycle tubes that he wants for the new slingshots we are working
on. And he reminds us, "Before we dey go to the market proper,
it be good if you give me dey money so de shop man no dey think
it be you who want dis for slingshot, otherwise he dey think, it
be worth more, or dat you and Reed be de ones with dey money,
and then it will be very dear."

The smell of the market is a mixture of pungent, sour, rotten,
sweet, fragrant, burnt rubber, burnt metal, yellow soap, and
talcum powder from the women traders. Everything but beads and
costume jewelry have an intentional or unintentional smell, due to
the lack of refrigeration. It must have been known how much will
sell regularly, or the rotten part would have gotten us all.

The hum of the voices — haggling and storytelling to the passers-by about the value of the items between rows of stalls, meandering around in different directions — stretch all the way to the beach, two to three miles away.

Finally, there is the level with the multi-colored clothing, the red cola-stained teeth of the mammies selling their produce, the taste of smoke from the charcoal brazier cooking stews, *Fou-fou, Gari,* bits of meat, curries, smoked fish, and plantain. Alassa knows where we are going. Soon we are in the bicycle section: wheels, frames, seats, horns, parts, paint — whatever you need, someone is selling it and someone else is buying it.

Alassa approaches one man with some red bicycle rubber shaped in a square, sitting in front of him. "Dis kind not be dey best kind to use for anything. You know dey ting be no good. It dey break every time you dey put on the bicycle-self. It not be fine-fine! If you get proper sense, you dey sell to me cheap."

The man looks at Alassa wearing his old shirt and worn-out clothes. "Who be this white pickens?" he asks. "Why dey be here?"

Alassa replies, "We come to see the market, we just wanted to look see. The way the whites how be they so … you dey know what I mean?"

The man says something in Hausa and smiles; Alassa says something back. I know it is a Hausa WaWa about white people, but I am more interested in getting a good price so I will have some allowance left over.

"Two shillings for that piece," Alassa says.

"No," says the man, "this be three- shillings quality, you feel it; it be number one red tube. If you no dey like red, why you no dey try black?" But Alassa waves the man on and goes on examining the other stalls. "Let us go another side, so dis man he no dey think we buy his red tube," Alassa says.

I tell Alassa I want to go down to the beach to watch the large canoes, cut from a single tree, unloading crates from the freighters.

It is quite a sight. Each African paddles as fast as he can in unison with the others when the large one-piece wooden canoe loaded with crates in the middle hits the point of a wave where the surf begins. Hopefully, each boat can catch the high point of a wave as it begins to break and ride the wave to the shore, but that does not always happen. Even though the coxswain at the back will yell to the paddlers to go faster, they can slip off the wave and get overturned by the next one, or the one behind might overturn them if their boat is not straight in the line of the force of the wave. Sometimes waves even bounce back from the shore to collide with those coming in.

The closer we get, I realize that these men are huge and have muscles like weightlifters. The reflecting tropical sun makes them seem silver at a distance, (like a bunch of silver surfers from the comic books even though the silver surfer comic books did not occur until 1966). But they work like crazy on the way in, even though there is a small crowd watching from the shore, who will fall down laughing if the boat goes over. The silver, glistening, muscle-bound paddlers just take the whole matter in stride, whichever way it goes. I thought think it looks like hard work. WaWa, West African longshoremen.

Anyway, after we watched six or seven boats, two of which go over and the cargo either sinks or floats to the beach, Alassa says we are going to return to the first man we had seen since he has what we want, and with some luck, because the afternoon is closing in, we might get our price. So, we go back and the man says, "I dey know you want my family to die of starvation, still I will let the matter be so." So we all go home happy that day, except perhaps for the merchant.

Alassa and I do not go to his farm area until the second time we live in Accra. I am not sure why; maybe Alassa thinks I will only be interested in bush hunting, or maybe we are both younger ourselves back in the previous tour of Accra.

In order to get where the villagers have their farms, you have to take a footpath across a small stream, up a small hill, and go another five hundred yards farther into the bush. All told, it is at least two miles away by foot. As we near the area, I notice there are fewer big trees and more thick or round bushes. The ground begins to turn color from red to brown to black. Apparently there is more water in the soil compared to the previously dusty footpath made firm by the slaps of many feet and sandals. Alassa has brought two tools with him, his machete and a homemade hoe that has a pick on one side and a flat, round blade on the other.

JULY 13, 1959

Alassa shows me his rows of cassava yam starts, each of which have been carefully put in a round castle of mud to grow up into a one- or two-pound tuber. Then it will be harvested and sold, eaten, or possibly traded for something else, either in the village or sold by his mother in the marketplace down in Accra. Alassa also has some groundnuts growing near the cassava yams. Alassa has some other yams growing, and I cannot tell if they are cassava or not. I do not know much about farming. Actually, I know what the various African foods taste like, but like looking in the meat section in the supermarket, I can only identify the obvious. Not wanting to betray my ignorance or insult Alassa about an activity that obviously takes up much of his time, I watch in silence as he hoes away weeds and small plants that are interfering with his plot of land.

When he asks me later why I was so silent, I say, "Dis be lots of work; it dey give you power to do other things." But I worry as

I say that the weather, the insects, or just the fact that as a cash crop yams are just a staple, will limit him to being a subsistence-level farmer.

Alassa looks at me intently and says, "Dis no be de matter; work self bring good *ju-ju*, even when de bad *ju-ju* want to destroy dis." We both laugh when he adds WaWa.

JULY 14, 1959

George Peters, a British boy, lives at 27 Tesano, a house farther up from ours. I call him the scorpion teenager. He catches scorpions at night when they come out from their hiding places. The scorpions are all over the road, looking for insects and small animals to eat. They come in two kinds. The black six-inch scorpions and the red three- to four-inch scorpions. They look just like baby lobsters, but they are poisonous and have a stinger, where a lobster has a webbed tail. The red ones are more poisonous than the black ones; the black ones use their claws to hang on to their prey and sting it more than once. George used to come around to the house with the red scorpions in his pockets.

One day, while Abel is bringing him an Orange Crush, he carefully puts his hand in his pocket and puts a red scorpion inside his palm. Then he unfolds his palm and shows Abel what he has in it. The first time he does this, Abel drops the soda on the floor in his hurry to get some distance between himself and George. The second time, Abel simply puts the Orange Crush at some distance. Abel told Mother about the scorpions, and Mother told George not to come over, since his only amusement seemed to be to scare everybody. George is more afraid of Mother than of the scorpions, so he does not return. The trick he uses is to capture the scorpions in bottles and then use tweezers to pull off their stingers. I am relieved, since I am not certain that the stingers will re-grow, the way lizard tails do if you shoot them off with a slingshot.

We get Mother to get the driver to take us to Labadi Beach. There my father's company has a house and small body boards for surfing. The beach house is a wooden house with a yellow thatched roof, made of concrete stilts. It has a bar inside. It is located at the extreme end of the beach from where people swim. A wooden bridge over a clear lagoon connects the beach to an island of sand, from which we swim out into the Atlantic surf. For hours, Reed and I will surf, going out as far as we can. There is a wicked undertow, so we have to be careful. Sometimes the first wave bounces back and we get caught in a sandwich between it and the next wave. One time, I got knocked out, and my mother, who is at the beach by chance, pulls me up by my hair. All in all, it is a superb way to get a freckled tan and have a wonderful time.

JULY 15, 1959

My mother is driving us back from Labadi Beach, where we have been surfing. She is in quite a hurry to get back, as she has to prepare for a dinner party at home. An African policeman suddenly jumps out of the bush by the side of the road and waves to Mother to stop. "Madame," he says, "you are going over the limit. But why?"

Without a smile or a second thought, my mother, pointing to the closed ashtray in the car, says, "I have a fire in the ash-tray, and I am rushing home to put it out."

I think this policeman thinks my mother is a bit WaWa or he has never heard this story before, so he waves us on.

JULY 18, 1959

On another trip to Labadi Beach, we are all jammed into the company car, six in the back, that is, we three children smelling of orange squash and curry, and three adults smelling faintly of gin and strongly of curry. It is Saturday — curry day and a day at the beach. In the front seat there are three adults and Coagie's girlfriend, Niki. An African policeman near the beach jumps out from the side of the road. "Master," he says to the driver, "Who dey own dis car?" All the adults immediately pointed to my dad, who is sitting in the front. "If you dey go to the Labadi Beach, full up like a mammy wagon, ten pounds is a fine for a car too full up. If you dey pay me fifteen pounds dash I no dey write you ticket." (A dash is a gift to expedite business.) Since Dad has been named owner of the car, he has to pay the dash. I think it is "jolly unfair" of the others who are British to do this. But later, when I tell Dad that it is "jolly unfair," he says that "jolly unfair" is a British expression and this business is *"yacatti,"* meaning "finished, no more at all, vanished out of reality." Though Dad can speak a bit of pidgin, I still think it is WaWa on the British side.

JULY 19, 1959

The white duplex house in Tesano has marigolds in the front yard, as well as a badminton court where Reed and I play. It is said, "Only mad folks and Englishmen go out in the noonday sun." Since Reed and I have been in school in England, we feel we are up to the problem, though almost everyone else (except our father and some of the Europeans at work) takes a nap in the afternoon. Reed and I like to play badminton at noon because the sun is right overhead. And if you hit the birdie (shuttlecock) straight up, then the sun has the tendency to blind the other person, and they'll miss by a mile. Reed and I play regularly at that time, and each of us specializes in the long, high, two-handed whack straight up as far as possible into the sun. As a result, our games have the tendency to look like two drunks falling out of a car. Some people say we play like fools or are WaWa. That's how we like it!

Mother has acquired a French poodle and named it Café, after Café au Lait, our cocker spaniel in Baimville. While we are away in school, Café has grown big enough to get his first haircut. Reed and I arrive just in time for that. Café has never had a haircut before, so when he returns home, he tries to prance around in his newly cut coat, with his balls of fur around his ankles and tail. But he doesn't get far before the Africans in the house begin to laugh at him. He runs outside with no better result. So he runs into my parents' bedroom and hides under the bed for two days. French poodles and haircuts. WaWa.

JULY 20, 1959

Since Dad and Mom, through our correspondence, know we are playing lawn tennis in England, Dad arranges for us to have tennis lessons when we get to Accra the second time. This time, unlike the scouts, we have no conflict over God Save the Queen and the Pledge of Allegiance. Our tennis instructor is a black American named Chris. Ghana is now independent, so a black man playing tennis is quite normal. The fact that he is Afro-American only indicates that the color barrier in tennis still needs to be broken. At first, Reed and I are very enthusiastic, but we have to work on our basics. The courts are clay, not grass, so all my cleverness to hit the grass just on the line, where it is slick and will sneak by my opponent, is useless. Clay is equally firm throughout, and the bounce is much higher. And since it is not the rainy season, the clay is hit with a burst of dust, but the dust does not confuse my opponent.

Chris has long arms and legs, and he moves like an antelope if I try to out-fox him by playing to another side of the court. We are cream puffs compared to him. So Reed and I go back to basics. A smooth forearm swing, a smooth backhand, moving up to the net after serving. This is great tennis in Ghana. Even so, Reed and I have a tendency to try to kill the tennis ball. We will start with a hundred tennis balls, but soon enough we will hit sixty-five tennis balls over the back fence. Ordinarily, you can do something about this, but Chris will talk about the snakes and how we can't just go behind the court and collect the tennis balls we have slammed or lobbed over the fence. So Reed and I will be forced to make an extra effort with smooth swings to keep the balls on the court. Every week we go for tennis, Chris will have a hundred tennis balls. Reed and I never ask how the tennis balls got back without the snakes attacking whoever retrieved them. Maybe it is Chris's *ju-ju*. WaWa tennis.

One afternoon, in our second Tesano house, Coagie and his girlfriend Niki are paddling around in the wading pool in the backyard. They spot a small green snake with brown patches slithering into the wading pool, so they splash out of the pool. Coagie goes to get the gardener, whose Christian name is John, but John bolts the scene when he sees the small snake swimming around the pool. He yells at Coagie to get Madame. So Coagie runs into the house, but Mom thinks he is crying wolf. In the meantime, Niki begins to wail, so Coagie, not dissuaded, runs back and arms himself with a plastic submarine from the wading pool and smashes the head off the snake. The snake is later determined by the neighbors to have been extremely poisonous, although it is not known for its aggression nor fortunately for its combat experience with plastic submarines. WaWa, Coagie.

Dad keeps a sailboat in Tempa Harbor, where we will go sailing on the weekends. One week, combining sailing and fishing, we put a pole over the side and catch a small barracuda, right near the swimming area. Sometime later, somebody told us about getting a six-footer in the same area. But it is usually too complicated to sail and fish at the same time, and if we get bored sailing, we can snorkel in the brand- new, unpolluted harbor. But usually we sail in the harbor area because of the heavy waves beyond.

Speaking of waves, sometimes we will go to the beaches up the coast. The undertow makes swimming too dangerous, but fishing canoes come in through the surf. Everyone gathers to watch. It is a source of great amusement to see who will turn over and who will not. "WaWa West Africa," they will say, whenever a boat keel goes up. The fish caught the night before will float to the sand, so that they are available for anyone.

JULY 21, 1959

At home we have a turkey and a monkey. Dad bought the turkey for Christmas dinner, but it never got eaten because the monkey gets loose and pulls all the feathers off its rear-end. So we have a bald-assed turkey that we consider too pitiful to eat.

I remember when the executives from New York, who are called firemen by my father, were trying to recover from the night before, and one of them goes to pick up the butter dish, when a small hand grabs it away. Before anyone can do anything, the monkey had climbed up the curtain with the butter dish in his hand, and then the poodle starts to bark at the monkey, so the monkey threw the butter in globs at the dog and all over the room, hitting the guests. I am not sure those two from New York ever volunteered to stay with us again. WaWa.

JULY 22, 1959

The scariest but also funniest thing happens. My parents went go out to a party in a bit of a mood. When they returned, they are deep in discussion with each other, while they park the car in the middle of the garage. In the morning, an irate night watchman is throwing a temper tantrum. When the translations are done, it turns out my parents have parked the car right over the sleeping night watchman; he is accusing them of trying to murder him. They feel he isn't doing his job. In the end, he agrees not to sleep in the garage.

Now that Gold Coast has become Ghana, many popular rumors circulate. To be sensitive to one, one needs to keep in mind its fullest sense. One of the most popular notions is that after independence, money will be dispensed to one and all, but given that the money has gone out of the country, this isn't particularly unreasonable. One of the less important rumors is that Kwame Nkrumah has put his name on Ring Road Circle in neon and that it is his fault that his name will flash at night on the "clouds many miles away." Another is that after he is disposed of, it will be necessary to dig a fifty-foot hole beneath his statue, so that his spirit will not have any ju-ju.

But Kwame Nkrumah is a great man. I remember sitting opposite his motorcade and seeing him go by, and feeling chills go up and down my spine. He is the Sam Adams or George Washington of his time, and no better leader with his vision of Pan-Africanism and charisma has appeared to this day. WaWa to Kwame.

JULY 30, 1959

After Reed and I leave Accra, Mom writes to us about getting Winnie the parrot. Winnie has been living with a Spanish couple. The husband is a freight handler for Pan-American, and they are about to be transferred. Once again, Dad and Mom's soft touch for animals comes into play, and Winnie moves into Tesano #2. She moves into the white duplex, along with the bald-assed turkey, the monkey, and Café the ironically black-haired poodle. Mom writes to tell us about Winnie's language capacity. It is a bit different than Mom thought, since she did not know all the languages Winnie did, or at least not the same vocabulary.

When Dad, Mom, and Coagie are in customs, about to leave Accra, a customs man notes all the animals they have with them and says, "This is a menagerie, Madame." Coagie bristles, believing he might lose the pets, though he never liked this monkey much, as he bites Coagie far too often. (And Coagie has not tried my strategy to bite the monkey back and show it all your teeth!). Mother brushes all of this aside, saying, "This is my family, and I won't leave without them." So Dad, Mom, Coagie, and the pets get on the plane.

When Dad, Mom, Coagie and the menagerie arrive in Lagos, Nigeria, the customs officials are a bit stiff at first. They ask for the required veterinary certificate of health, particularly for the parrot! Mom reaches into her purse and hands the man a document without looking at it. He studies it for some time and, then asks in an incredulous tone, "Are you going to eat this bird?" Mother snatches back the paper to find it is a recipe for "Chicken Hawaiian" that a friend had given her on their departure. Despite Mom's explanations and protests that both the monkey and the parrot are actually Nigerian and they are repatriating them in the interest of Nigeria, the official puts Winnie into custody. And It is only with much pull and some dash (cash) that Dad succeeds in getting the bird and monkey back from Lagos customs.

KADUNA, NIGERIA

JULY 1, 1960

To get to Kaduna, you have to take a plane to Kano. Kano is surrounded on one side by fields of groundnuts (peanuts) and the other by the Emir of Kano's palace, which covers a large portion of the city. The Emir has a family dynasty that goes back some six hundred years. Dad tells us this on the way to our new home in Kaduna. Dad also explains that Kaduna is the British Administrative center of northern Nigeria, so it has become a commercial center too, during the British rule. The camel trains we see on the way are going to places such as Sokoto, where the Sultan of Sokoto lives in his palace. I know that these people are polygamous, which seems nice to me, since a new wife will help the first wife with the children and work around the house. Still, after Dad tells me the Sultan of Sokoto (the head of the Hausa people) has an entire polo team made up of his sons, I have to wonder when he has time to do anything else. It seems like a lot of wives and sons to me.

My first impression of Kaduna is like the one of Egypt. The peanuts stacked in pyramids lay for miles along the roadside. It is arid country and is on the trade route to Khartoum across the desert.

When Reed and I get to Kaduna, there is neither sight nor sound of the monkey. This is a different monkey, not Monkmonk from Kumasi, so I say nothing. Reed has no interest either. Coagie says nothing, since the monkey has bitten him too many times. Dad takes Reed and me aside and explains that while in Aba, the monkey had run away and Mom is upset about it, so we are not to bring it up. We both feel fine about that.

Our parents make a point of taking us over to the club. While we are recalcitrant and shy, it turns out our fears are misplaced. There is a billiards room, a poolroom, (the British call it a pool room because they play pool differently from billiards) and a swimming pool. In the morning, there is horseback riding; in the afternoon, we play pool, swim, or play field hockey. Our hockey team is mixed in gender, color, and age, so we are an exception in the league. We play all-black or all-white teams. It is the white teams who are a pain. Usually they make the mistake of not taking us seriously. I play goalie, so I remember well how the white engineer takes six shots, and by luck, I block them all. He is so mad, he throws his hockey stick on the ground and the referee nearly throws him out of the game. My voice is just beginning to turn, so I yell, "Come on, teenagers," which is quite non-British.

JULY 5, 1960

Tsetse flies are as big as horseflies, up to the size of a quarter. It is reported that the reason that there are no dairy cows in northern Nigeria or West Africa, for that matter, is tsetse flies. They can also bite people if they chose to. They do not like the taste of people much, but it is okay periodically if the tsetse fly cannot find

Hausa cows or wild cows to drive crazy with their attacks. Hausa cows only give enough milk for their calves.

One afternoon, we go swimming. As I go to the high diving board of the pool for my turn in the diving contest, I am not thinking about tsetse flies, though one is thinking of me. I stand still and put my arms at my side and walk to within a foot of the end of the board, pausing again to focus. I run to the end of the board and jump off to catch the bounce of the board. As I do, something large and ugly lands at the end of my nose. Keeping my focus on my dive, I ignore it. Then the pain begins to spread all over my face. My hands immediately move to kill the quarter-sized monster. Of course, when my hands move to my face, my dive turns into a horizontal belly flop from the highest board. The water nearly drowns the judges, and I crawl out as the pain from my stomach spreads and the center of my nose throbs. There is a red swelling in the middle of my nose. As for the tsetse fly, I figure it gets full points from all those other tsetse flies it meets that day. WaWa for tsetse flies. Bad *ju-ju* for stomach flops from the high board. Still, I won the breaststroke contest.

JULY 7, 1960

The days are one thing but the nights are something else. Each parent, including the Lebanese, will make a different house available every night. The parents will go out and have us chauffeured to a house, and if we wanted to drink or dance, we can do one or the other. And because there is American (Armed Forces Radio) in the area, we get all the Top Pops. My mother tries to tell me the music is just like "Volaré," which is just adapted from Italian music, but Elvis just doesn't seem Italian to me. Anyway, it is a wonderful life to live, and our party group is quite sensational in its international composition of Irish, Lebanese, English, Americans, and Africans.

JULY 8, 1960

Captain John Brown, or "Patch" as we call him, used to come over for drinks to our house at Kaduna. He usually comes in a military khaki shorts uniform and wears the same black patch over his blind eye; I often wondered what it looked like underneath. He looks like a military version of the Hathaway shirt man, but I feel he takes this one- eye business a bit too far. One afternoon, I am flying my kite two hundred feet over the house, and he offers to shoot it down. Since I believe he cannot do it after drinks, and that my kite is far away, I defer to his request. He gets out an Enfield rifle he has in the trunk of his car. Loading up, he puts the rifle to his good eye and shoots a series of holes around the left center of my kite, and it crashes into the nearby shrubbery. Captain Brown is pleased with himself. I am crushed at my own stupidity. I know that every time he visits in the future, he will volunteer to do the same thing. The best I can hope for is to go to the club when he is coming over or just tell him that it is pure luck. But, having a lot of pride, I think WaWa to the one-eyed British military officer and I stay at the club when I know he is coming over. When he drops in unexpectedly, I go upstairs to my room until it is dark.

His circle of shots has been only to one side of the kite, so the kite still flies with a tilt and a wobble. One evening, when my annoyance gets the better of me, I put the kite back up. Since it wobbles with its repairs, I think I will surely prove my point this time. Later, Patch shoots the Balsa wood crossbar of the kite to shreds, and the whole kite is destroyed. He thinks it is funny. "Hey, young man, what do you think of that?" he asks.

"Super," I say, telling myself I should have stuck to my first thought about one-eyed British military officers.

JULY 9, 1960

The house is made of glass, for the most part, so all activities are visible inside the compound. It is here that we have a washer man, or what some call the laundry man, who comes to the house periodically. In between the kitchen and the main house, there is a room with two large sinks, and a corridor wide enough to get the food from the kitchen to the main house. On the other side, there is another room where the washer man can do the ironing. Dad, Mom, and Coagie have been living in Aba, Nigeria, before they moved to Kaduna, and not everything had moved with them. The washing machine did not arrive until some three months later. John, which is the Christian name of the washer man, has not had the pleasure of working with a washing machine, as he tells Mother. "This machine be fine, fine," he says. My mother agrees with him and shows him how to operate it.

All seems well until my mother notices the washer man takes the same amount of time he had in the past to do the laundry. So one day my mother goes to observe what is going on. There she finds John loading the washing machine. Then he proceeds to put in the soap and turn it on. As soon as he has done that, he pulls up a chair and sits down next to the machine. When the machine has gone through its cycle, he puts the washed clothing into the sink. He repeats this procedure until all the washed clothes are in the sink with the understanding that only then will they be ready to take to the line for drying.

My mother watches this procedure with some astonishment. So she asks John if he understands what the purpose of the washing machine is. "Yes, Madame, dis machine, he dey do de work I do before," he replies. My mother asks if he understands that this convenience means that he can do the washing more quickly. "No, Madame," he says, "Dis machine give me more time off when I come for your side." That is why he likes it so much.

Coagie has an African friend, Simon, whom he goes around with in Kaduna. One of Coagie's and Simon's favorite places to go is the Kaduna market. This market, like most African markets, has a fresh meat area. Since there is no refrigeration, and the weather is tropical, some meat goes bad and some parts of the meat are not marketable. Rotten meat means vultures. Vultures have earned their reputation as bad news, garbage-disposal birds the easy way — in looks and otherwise. They are not small; a full-blown, well-fed, bald-headed vulture has a five- to six-foot wingspan. Their beaks are curved, and they charge and snap when offal is available, but otherwise they are cowards. Coagie and Simon will throw sticks and stones at the vultures, hoping to get them to fly. Ugliness has its princely side, for once vultures get it together to fly, and their ugliness becomes a brown effortless move in circles. At first, they also look like they cannot rise, flapping their wings awkwardly as though they may crash. However, they are so lazy that they use the slightest updraft to circle upward, freezing like a brown boomerang going up around and around in perfect circles, and they can go until they are nothing but tiny spots in the sky. Their beady black eyes can see movement or lack of it, or the slow death of movement or an animal from hundreds of feet up. Up close, you can see the black lice on their baldheads; memorable and useful birds really. WaWa.

After that exercise, Simon and Coagie go for their favorite refreshment: fresh sugar cane, chopped by machete after selecting your piece. Sugar cane drips with pure 100 percent cane sugar juice. As you chew it, it becomes like a combination of a cane made of powdered sugar, wet like a watermelon, and chewy so you have to work it slightly to get the juice. There is only one problem with this part of the trip. No matter how much negotiation Coagie and Simon try and how they complain that the cost will ruin them and their families forever (to the amusement of the sellers), they have to pay the money sooner or later. Sugar cane is not free.

JULY 10, 1960

One day, Coagie and Simon go home on a different route from the usual way. Along the way, they find a small patch of sugar cane growing near the road and a nearby well. Thinking it is their lucky day; the two rush to the compound and come back with a sharp knife. When they return, they wait until nobody is coming, and using the serrated edge of the knife, they cut down three times as much as they ordinarily ate at the market. Up in Coagie's room, they cut up the cane, cutting out square blocks to chew and then swallow. Both of them chew and swallow until their faces are covered with a film of sticky cane- sugar water. Simon says he has to go home, so Coagie says fine. "This he be great day, Simon, now you can keep more money for dey chocolates, dis be fine-fine past Takoradi self."

Simon says "Laufia," meaning *good-bye* or *see you later,* and leaves. Coagie lies down on his bed to read comics. Half an hour later, Coagie thinks the bed is rocking back and forth. A pain starts in his stomach. Suddenly, he is throwing up all over the bed, the sheets, and the covers. Coagie runs to the bathroom, but the damage has already been done. He still has a terrible stomach ache. The sugar cane had been far too green to eat. Sugar cane is not free if you steal it; it has its price and its bad ju-ju WaWa.

When Coagie is in the third grade in the British private school in Kaduna, his *ju-ju* works on the teacher. The students are preparing a concert. It is to be held in an open-air pavilion with only a thatched roof to keep off the sun. Coagie and his class practice the songs over and over again for the benefit of the anticipated audience of parents and government officials. Coagie, in his usual experimental approach, tries singing the songs in different tones. At first, the teacher cannot figure out who is doing this, but when she does, she stops the singing and asks Coagie to sing along normally. Finally, Coagie acquiesces. Still, the teacher does not seem pleased. "Young man, please wait after the practice is over," she says.

Coagie waits after the others are gone. The teacher puts her hand on his shoulder and says, "Young man, I don't think opera is in your future; it will be best for all concerned if you simply mouth the words to the songs as we go along." Coagie worries that Dad and Mom might notice this, but after the concert they are as enthusiastic as the others. It seems he can avoid telling our parents certain things.

As Coagie further explains when he and the 'rents lived in Aba, he got away with certain matters only because he has good ju-ju. First of all, Dad and Mom let him swim in the Niger River, where the current is strong. He swims with the aid of one or two friends to the raft up-stream and then drift to the one down-stream and then to the riverbank. The river has a water-borne disease that can make you go blind. But the 'rents let him do it. He is the youngest, and we two older boys have worn out the 'rents in their do's and don'ts.

Then there is Coagie's method of proving that he has brushed his teeth every night. He will wait until it is the cocktail hour, and then he will go to the bathroom and put a dab of toothpaste on his tongue and breathes on the 'rents. Between the smell of the cocktails and the toothpaste, all is fine; a little dab will do you. WaWa.

JULY 11, 1960

When Dad gets sick in Kaduna, the house seems unusually quiet. No parties for us, no dinner parties for them. The time seems to go backwards. Mom gets quiet, Reed and I get worried. The doctor visits frequently. After the first tour in Accra, Reed and I know people might die. And in Kumasi, it seems more difficult than clear about the experience. What we do know is that

Dad is not in the hospital, just in bed, quartered and quarantined, and not at work, day after day. Mom does not exactly tell us what Dad is sick from. Somehow, I think it is jaundice, yellow fever, or malaria, the last of which you get when not taking your quinine (malaria pills). In the case of the malaria pills, Dad is not like Coagie, who has to have his crushed up and mixed with a spoon of sugar. So I rule that out. I think yellow fever seems possible, for no better reason that I think that if you are white and living in the tropics, you can get it, because if you have a tan, you might not know or notice it when you get yellow. Then Jaundice seems like a possibility, because Dad loves shellfish, and I have heard Mom tell Dad to watch his shellfish consumption because of that. On the other hand, we are not far from the Sahara, and we don't have access to much in the way of shellfish, so jaundice doesn't make sense. So where will Dad find the shellfish? When Dad is better in a couple of weeks, Mom says it has been jaundice. I still have no idea where Dad had found the shellfish, but my dad is resourceful and has strong ju-ju

JULY 12, 1960

Probably the most intelligent member of the house is Winnie the parrot. She is smart enough that when she is let out of her cage, she will go to the bathroom. When Dad and Mom have a dinner party or a cocktail party at the house, Winnie's cage will be put in the corner of the living room with a cloth over it. Winnie will usually sleep through dinner parties, but cocktail parties are more challenging. Of course, if Winnie awakens, what happens will mystify the guests. All over the living room, you will hear cursing from a Hausa person, an Ebo person, a Ga person, a Spanish person, a Portuguese person, a Twi person, a Fulani person, and last but not least, an English-speaking person. People will look around to see who is being so vulgar in so many languages, but see no one around and so they are upset at the party. Sometimes, if Winnie creates an impression that she is a number of speakers, she will raise tensions at the party, because not all these groups have the same opinion of each other. Mom will signal with her hands to be quiet, but Winnie cannot see this and will carry on. Then, Mom will take the cloth off Winnie's cage and everyone will laugh. Then Mom will have the two stewards and the small boy lug Winnie's heavy cage upstairs to the small guest room. WaWa, Winnie.

One of Winnie's other favorite tricks is to call the dogs. When she is out on the floor, she whistles for the dogs, and the dogs come in. Then one of the dogs lifts his leg and pees on the bird. But this does not stop the old bird. Her favorite habit is to get out of the cage, claw up the furniture, perch on my shoulder, pull on my earlobe, and say, "Give me a kiss, pretty girl." She has a strong beak and is very persistent about getting attention. When you say, "Okay, Winnie," she will bend her head forward and you have to scratch between the feathers on her neck. Unless you want this to go on and on, you have to move her slowly back to her cage. Of course, she complains on the way back to her cage by using language that would make a sailor blush. Dear old Winnie is still living in Kaduna, learning new words today, and having her neck scratched by those who let her out of her cage. Winnie's other habit is that if you let her out of her cage, she immediately decides to relieve herself, or if you pick her up on your arm, she will do it there, which is quite a warm shock for the person.

We also have a donkey, known as Donk-donk. Usually friendly, he threw my father right on his head when Dad first tried to ride him. My father has a cart made so that Reed, Coagie, and I can go to the club, but it is faster to walk. Donk-donk is never in a hurry, and likes to eat his way there. That is fine, except there is no harness- maker in the area, so there is no way to do much more than strap him in. After a few kicks, he gets used to the thing, but the reins are not much incentive to keep his sense of direction or speed.

Two things about our glass house stand out. One is that although we get robbed, the night watchman shoots the burglar in the fanny with a poisoned arrow. The burglar thinks this is unfair, and comes to complain about it, because he is more than halfway across the fence when he gets hit, but he gets no sympathy for his medical bills. Second is that in the mornings, the radio will be tuned to the local Muslim show, and it is very African for me to hear the music and watch the steward sweep the house.

JULY 15, 1960

Early morning, a Hausa man arrives. He looks beaten and dusty. His robe is ripped, and the blue dye in the background of the white is faded, showing that the robe is old and has been washed many times. He shows up at nine o'clock on Saturday morning. Only we boys are up; the 'rents are still asleep. It is, after all, a Saturday, and they have gotten back late from a dinner party. Dad will later mention that it is awkward because the Hausa people do not imbibe alcohol, due to their religious beliefs, but the Europeans do, so the two crowds mix like vinegar and water or squash and scotch. The man at our door tells John, the first steward, that he is a diamond merchant and he has some valuable uncut diamonds to sell Dad and Mom.

By lunchtime, the 'rents have refused to buy the stones four times. The price, however, is beginning to drop, even as the stories of the woes in the man's life and those of his family increase. The 'rents are really not interested, and John goes back in the yard periodically in the afternoon to tell the man, "it no be good ting." The man persists and persists, wandering around the yard until the dogs begin to think he is some new African come to work in the compound.

Consistently in the morning, and less so in the afternoon, the donkey has rubbed him from behind, hoping for cigarette butts which the donkey loves to eat, but has no luck. Only Winnie the parrot has been oblivious to this man's presence. Finally, my mother's "poor old soul" theory takes over, and Dad's practical sense that the African seems as if he will sleep on the porch unless something is done goes into effect. So Dad goes out (and we boys with him) to help negotiate as low a price as possible. The man sticks to his story that the stones are uncut diamonds, smuggled from South Africa. When the price finally gets below those of any real diamonds and is bankrupting the man's entire extended family, Dad buys the stones, and the man goes away. Dad does not believe they are diamonds. He has them examined, and they are moonstones, a semi-precious, but hardly rare, stone. When Neil Armstrong says, "One small step for man, one giant leap for mankind" from the moon, I wonder if our desperate, persistent Hausa man is still selling moonstones in Kaduna. WaWa.

JULY 18, 1960

Going to the zoo in Kaduna is as typical as going to a zoo anywhere in Africa. On one particular occasion of visiting, Reed and I are not that interested, but Coagie is thrilled. The first animals we see in a small compound are dikers. Male dikers have small cuts on their faces. If you place your hand in the cages, they will rub up and down against your hand. This leaves a sticky, white jelly all over your hand. The jelly is to leave a mark on you, indicating you are in their territory. Reed and I are old hands at this from missionary school, so we keep our hands out of their cage. Coagie knows that but does it anyway until Mom tells him to leave them alone.

Reed and I go over to see the chimpanzee in his cage. We ask an African man looking on with us, "But why dis monkey have de small house?"

He replies, "After dis monkey do grow old, past thirty-five-self, it not be fine, fine at all, it be cranky. They don't let it play with de others cause they not get proper sense." I wonder if that is why my parents get so cranky with me from time to time. WaWa.

Then Mom's commanding voice is heard. "Come here now, Reed and Billy. We are going to buy a bunch of bananas for the other animals." We fall in line and join Mom and Coagie. As we begin to walk with the bananas, an unknown drumming sound begins to fill the air. Coagie begins to scream. Reed and I freeze in terror. An ostrich is running with its head stretched out and its feet pounding away, straight towards us. Mother looks up to see the beady-eyed, flat-headed pounding bird and stands her ground in her usual fashion. Many people yell, "Drop the bananas, Madame, drop the bananas!" So Mother does just that, and we children run in the opposite direction. Meantime, the ostrich runs away with the bananas. Everyone laughs, because we had not known about the menacing ostrich. WaWa.

Reed and I are in for a second surprise. The camels are just hobbled in the zoo yard. So Reed and I go right up to them. The first thing we notice is that their smell is similar to garbage fermenting in the sun. We also notice that their stomachs seem to be constantly growling. But the biggest surprise is the least anticipated. If the camels do not like you, they can do something about that, something Reed and I discover the hard way. Reed and I get spat on with the foulest globs of yellow halitosis spit you can imagine. We have to rush home early, take long, hot baths, and put on clean clothes.

JULY 19, 1960

Mom's WaWa and her ju-ju do not always work for her. The cook, whose Christian name is David, is examining the capons Mother has brought home from the Kingsway store. "Madame," he says, "dis bird de eggs here be too small; someone have stolen de regular size eggs of dis bird." So Mother goes to the Kingsway store and asks for the manager, and repeats David's complaints. "But, Madame," the manager says, "small bird can only give you small eggs." And for once Mom has nothing to say. WaWa.

JULY 20, 1960

Finally, there is the visit of Lady Graham Bell, the governor's wife. Just as my mother is putting away the swearing parrot, Lady Bell arrives in the limo and is surrounded by barking dogs. But it is the donkey that comes in from behind her and nudges her in the butt, which surprises her. The lady is smoking a cigarette. The donkey wants to get the cigarette butts from the ashtray in the house, which is his favorite reason to come into the house. Well, needless to say, it is her shortest visit in town, and we get a reputation for it.

Sally and Mary O'Hern, non-identical Irish twins, are my secret crushes on my vacation in Kaduna. I am still involved in the world of Donk-donk, Winnie the parrot, the dogs, my two brothers, and the 'rents, especially worrying about Dad's illness. Most of the time, the world is like the glass house. You can see through it to the other side, including its desert mirages. But there is another reality beyond the glass house, where you can see the comings and goings of people like actors on a stage, but I can only be in the audience in that reality when it comes to Sally and Mary. They are fifteen and a half. I am barely thirteen years old. I am shorter and stubby, with a rear end that you can place a beer on and not fear that it will fall off. My complexion, even with a tan, has the beginnings of pimples so common in adolescence.

I can only talk in passing with Sally and Mary at the parties or yell support for them at the field hockey games or win a swimming contest medal in front of them. I am a two-bit player in the background of their beauty. Their beauty is a royal, romantic possibility with incredible character that seems out of reach but not out of my pangs of desire.

Torture is in all directions, if anyone finds out that I, the short, pudgy, prepubescent has the nerve to romanticize about Sally or Mary O'Hern, then minimally I will turn a permanent lobster red, despite a tropical tan and be forced to take meals of bread and water, under a rock.

The torture is doubly intensified by the fact that not only are they not identical, but that I love one on one day and the other on the next. I dream of them in the daytime, with or without mirages, in the evenings, with or without their presence, and in the night, I even come within arms' dancing distance of one or the other at the club or at the night parties. Each time I see one, I will discover something in her favor and each time I see the other, I discover something new about her.

Since Kaduna is on the Saharan border, you can see mirages, and I will think, "This is a mirage that must go away. Maybe it will rain, and my feelings will cool off, or I will be able to choose one of them. Can I at least stop the sweet, throbbing pain, like when you push your gums hard and it hurts and hurts, but you want to push at it again and again?"

In the meantime, I have been describing the secret red scarlet red key as though I am the center of it. No, really it is the twins; they do it without effort and make it look like an act of grace, though it is murder for me.

By posture, Mary is not second. She carries herself like a Nigerian woman, carrying a huge tin of water with only a small circle of cloth on the head, with a firm upper torso, whereas Sally has more bounce to her posture.

Mary is the long- red- haired one. She is like a Nigerian Hausa aristocrat. The light of her laughter always passes her off as having a serious side too. She drinks scotch or champagne if there is any, otherwise only scotch with two ice cubes. Mary lets go of her reserve when it comes to horseback riding. She rides between the motion of the horse and the wind. Her red hair becomes a ripple of red, flashing to gold.

JULY 27, 1960

Sally can take the worst at its best. In many field hockey games, we will be two to three goals behind, against a team that seems quite invincible. Sally will calmly get the ball in mid-field and walk, dance, or move around players who think they have her stopped all the way to shoot a goal. Then she repeats the process. All-white teams often try to knock her down the next time around. These enthusiasts might indeed find themselves with a crack on their ankles when there is a struggle for the ball, which causes them to leave the field for a while, while their team plays short- handed.

Mary reserves her compliments in a way that points out the undiscovered beauty of ordinary things. In field hockey, it seems as if it is like some effortless, ordinary event when Sally passes to Mary, and Mary strokes the ball into the goal as if the goalie is on vacation, while the goalie is making every desperate action to crush her and stop the goal.

Sally provides counsel and friendship for the other teenage girls. Mary, on the other hand, is the vision of what teenage girls imagine someone at seventeen act: poised on the threshold of womanhood.

This continual and crushing tragedy is assisted by one final awkward fact: I have a dancing partner, Sarah, in my age group who helps me win dance contests. Just my luck that Sarah, a thin English girl, has a crush on me. She insists on telling me what the older girls are saying, to show that she belongs to their age group.

Between what Sarah tells me and what I imagine, it is clear I am only a wisp of a ghost in a mirage outside the reality of my dear loves. It is a Kaduna WaWa for me this summer, as I go from fish to fowl about girls and women. "But why dis ting be so?"

At this point, my brothers and I are separated. Reed stays on at school in England, Coagie stays with my parents, and I am sent on alone to a school in Switzerland. WaWa West Africa.

SWITZERLAND

As the plane rises into the hot, shimmering air at Kano, the nearest airport to Kaduna, I feel pangs of remorse about leaving the twins, the family, and Africa. A combination of fear and a sense of adventure soon overtake my first feelings. What will Switzerland be like? Will I be accepted by the students of my new school, Beau Soleil ("beautiful sun" in French)? Will I have friends who do not get into boxing matches with me, like Blakelock in Copthorne School in England?

There is also the excitement of seeing Switzerland for the first time. As the orange sun sinks over the scruffy yellow desert and over the pyramid-shaped mounds of peanuts near Kano as they turn into brown patches, I take my pillow and press it against the vibrating window of the four-engine Super G Constellation airplane and gradually fall into the uneasy twilight between sleep and rest. The stewardess apparently decides not to wake me for dinner. It is three o'clock in the morning when the angle of the plane's descent and the pitch change of the motors along with the noise of the wheels being lowered, awake me. My stomach is aching for some food. We have landed in Algiers.

As I exit the plane, I see them in the airport lights — soldiers, soldiers standing at attention in long rows, right up to the airport customs and waiting room. What is going on? Except for those passengers getting off at Algiers, we in transit are not going to find out in the empty transit room, guarded by two more soldiers.

The soldiers standing at attention holding guns at three o'clock in the morning make a vivid impression on me. My stomach ache seems to have vanished. After forty- five minutes on an uncomfortable chair, a customs official waves us back down the corridor of soldiers onto the plane. I want to wave as if I am a departing dignitary, but I have second thoughts about doing so. The returning passengers seem half- asleep, and the soldiers, well, I think they will not leave their position at attention, so I just climb up the ramp and back into the plane.

Years later, I realized I had landed in the middle of the colonial war of independence, in which the Muslim majority were fighting soldiers from the French Foreign Legion. Of course, the last point may not be so, but at that hour and in their discipline, they might have been the Foreign Legion!

The Super G Constellation flies on into the early hours of dawn. The orange sun rises again, this time over the blue Mediterranean. Off in the distance is either Spain or Italy. Breakfast is served, and I wolf down toast, powdered eggs smothered with cheese, and rich, thick cups of cocoa, as fast as the stewardess can bring it. This cocoa is from Nestlé, a Swiss company, which is my first WaWa in Switzerland.

After about four hours, I see mountains in the distance, and the stewardess tells me they are the Pyrenees and that we are two hours from Geneva. Soon I can see a blue spot in between the snow-capped mountains. It is Lake Geneva! The plane goes down to the lake and turns to land at the Geneva airport.

I get out of the plane, wondering who will be there at the airport to meet me. I go through customs, and then hear my name over the loudspeaker, "Coughlan, *Monsieur* Coughlan." I think that is probably me, so I go to the information desk and show my passport. *"Oui, oui,"* the clerk says. She looks at the spelling a couple of times and, then points to a stocky, tweed-coated Swiss gentleman and says, "Go see that gentleman. He is here to pick you up."

So I walk over to the gentleman and he takes my passport and ticket to collect my luggage from the carousel. He says, *"Bon Noveau élève suivez moi"* I say I do not speak French, but he is already collecting my bags and rushing out of the customs door to a nearby Volkswagen. There he puts my passport on the roof of the car and signals me to jump into the front seat. He throws my luggage in the back, jumps in, and we go off, speeding down the road. A moment later, I see my passport flying off the roof. Now I think I will be in Switzerland forever, as I will never be able to get out without a passport. So I shout to the man, "Passport, passport," pointing to the road, but he just smiles and drives faster down the cobbled streets. He cannot understand what I am talking about, and he is in a big hurry to get somewhere.

Fifteen minutes later, I see why he is in such a hurry. We are on a field surrounded by European cars, and a soccer match is about to begin. Quickly, he signals to me to sit on the bench, while he strips down to a soccer uniform underneath his clothes. Then he runs out into the field to join his teammates, just before the whistle blows to start the game. I am a bit relieved; at least I am not being kidnapped, even if the passport has flown off the roof. I sit worrying about my passport and waiting to settle into my new school.

Finally, the game is over. I gather from his attitude that his side has won. I mention, "Passport, passport." He thinks I want to see it so he goes looking for it in his jacket pocket, where he thinks he has kept it, but he can't find it. I point to the roof of the car and mimic the action of the passport flying off the roof of the car. He laughs and says something in French, which sounds something like *police*. I wonder if the police will hold me for not having the passport. But as I am thinking about that, he says *"Allez, Allez"* and points to the car. I get in. I think we will go back and look for the passport, but no, we speed up the coast around Lake Geneva. He drives like a maniac. I cling to the round plastic ring in the front by the passenger side of the Volkswagen.

At Lausanne, he makes a left that I see zigged and zagged up the mountain until I cannot see its end. The road is now half the size it was before and has many blind corners. Monsieur Lapart's tactic is not to slow down but to sit on his horn. I notice at corners that are virtual cliffs down the mountains that there are white crosses on the slopes, some with pictures or flowers on them. So I bring them to Fritz's attention, and he replies in broken English, "Dead ones." I figure that is the quaint Swiss way of marking deadly accidents. Not that that has any effect on the teacher. He just laughs again at my curiosity and keeps on driving like a bandit flying from a bank robbery.

I must have turned pale to the point that my freckles are standing out. Monsieur Lapart notices this and takes a hand off the wheel and slaps me on the back a few times, as if to comfort me. WaWa dead drivers. Just then, we come around a corner, and there is a herd of cows crossing the road. Monsieur Lapart sits on the horn, rolls the window down, and begins a rapid-fire discussion in French with the farmer. Whatever he says works. The farmer uses his stick on the cows to encourage them across the road. By now, we have passed through Vevey and Villeneuve and are close to our destination, Villars-sur-Ollon — the top resort village on the mountain where Beau Soleil is located.

Finally, we arrive at the tall concrete school, which is painted white. Tennis courts lay at the far end, with a small playground on one side and an open gymnasium at the other end. It is four stories on the side that goes down the mountain and three stories on the street side.

Monsieur Lapart takes my bags into the hall and up the stairs to the boys' dormitory. There he puts me in with a seventeen-year-old Cuban-American named Alex who is six feet tall and weighs 180 pounds and has a twin brother Steve of the same build and weight. "Welcome," says Alex., "They probably put you in with me temporarily so you can get used to the place."

It turns out Fritz Lapart is the gymnastics teacher for the boys. Thus, the general sports fanatic had picked me up. Monsieur Lapart speaks no English, only French and German. He often takes a group of older boys to his soccer games, besides teaching us gymnastics and tennis, and when the weather is bad, we play ping-pong. In the winter, he teaches skiing to the beginners. He lives for his gymnastics lessons and his soccer team. He is not a fast player, but as a halfback, he is like a tank cruising the field, getting the ball and outrunning the competition. At school, rumor has it that he and Madame Antoinette Fresche have a romance going. She is the gym teacher, as well as the dance and music teacher for the girls.

SEPTEMBER 2, 1960

With Alex as my roommate, I quickly find my way around the school, as well as learning all the gossip about the students and the teachers. Alex tells me that the upper school I am in has about twenty students who are boarders and there are ten 'townies." Brothers Jacque and Jean Pierre are training for the Olympics in skiing, and in between train at gymnastics. They speak no English and are in the Swiss-French classes taught by

Madame Marguerite Bouviere and Monsieur Rudolph Rennard, who teaches math to the French and German students, and also teaches the English students math and tennis.

There are two other English-speaking boys with us — Tom from New York City and Harry from New Jersey, besides Alex, Steve, and me. Alex tells me about the French boys, Jacques, Pierre, Petre, Marc Henri, Tomas, and Alain, about whom he will tell me more later. They make up the rest of the male teenagers, who are French and German speakers. But all of them can speak French. Alex says he is teaching them English in terms of how to pick up American tourist girls, who fill the resort town in the winter. Then he goes through the English-speaking girls, living in the dorms just across the roof. To get to the girls' dorms, there is a slide down to their window, he assures me. Susan, at only eleven, is too young but is a sweet, cute blonde; Karen, who is fourteen, is jailbait, he says, but I don't ask what that means. Ellen and Mary are two wallflower friends from New Jersey and Long Island. Mary and Nancy are Alex and Steve's interests "to do it," since they are sixteen and seventeen. I do not ask more about "to do it," figuring I will hear more later. Then there are Pepper and Salter, two other Americans who are too young and skinny, Alex tells me. "Watch out for Ellen," he says. When I ask why, he just laughs and says, "You'll find out." Then he says there are Susanne, Bridgette, Jeanne, Simone, and Violette, but he thinks they are too stuck -up because they are not interested in learning English, especially what he and Steve want to teach anatomically.

Fortunately, I have read *100 Ways to a More Powerful Vocabulary*, so I figure out what he means. I am impressed. I have been in a single-sex boarding school before and do not realize that girls can be a new subject to major in. WaWa, girls. Of course, I have heard about crushes, but Alex is talking as though the facts of life can be experienced more directly, and as long as I do not mess with his or Steve's interests, he is going to let me into the world of male teenage knowledge about girls.

I am thrilled, but then Steve comes in and asks Alex if he has told me why they are there in Switzerland. "No," says Alex.

"Well, you had better," says Steve. Then he asks me how old I am.

"Thirteen going on fourteen," I say.

"Well," he says, "you look small and immature for your age. I'll bet you are no more than twelve." I turn red while they laugh so hard, they both fall on Alex's bed.

"Well," says Steve, "you can tell him what you want, but he is not going to the showing tonight."

"Okay, brother," says Alex, "but I figure to tell him why we are here."

"Fine," says Steve, "you can tell him what you want, but he is too much of a shrimp for the showing; however old he claims to be, that's only for mature teenagers."

I go from a feeling of acceptance to a feeling of deep uncertainty. Why the mystery about being in school, and what is this "'showing'" I am being excluded from?

Alex begins to talk, and I hang on his every word. "Bill," he says, "Steve and I had a number of brushes with the law in Miami. Each of us has a long juvenile rap sheet. Do you know what that is?" I nod to avoid breaking up the flow of the conversation. "Well," he continues, "the last time we are in front of a judge, he said that our father will not be able to get us out on probation the next time round. And that he will send us into the army or to jail as adult offenders. So, our father says that the only thing he can do with us is to send us to a Swiss school to cool off. So, we are here."

Then, Alex goes on to explain that his father has a jewelry store in Miami, Florida and sells imported Swiss jewelry, and he knows what the Swiss police are like. Alex's father had explained to Steve and Alex that the Swiss police are very slick, and they use corporal punishment whether or not you are an American. In other words, they will take you out behind the jail and cane you if you give them any trouble. By now, I am thinking about my passport and wondering if Alex is telling me a story or not, but I let it be; I still want to know what this "'showing'" is about that I am excluded from. So I muster up my courage and ask Alex.

"Well," says Alex, "since you have the nerve to ask, I will tell you, but you will still not go." Alex goes on to explain that he and Steve have told the other English-speaking older teenagers that they have the biggest physical builds in the whole school, and word got out to the French-speaking teens who challenged the Americans — Steve and Alex — to prove it. They say that they will send two of their best and Alex and Steve will represent America's honor. So they have accepted the challenge. Hence, the showing is on this very day. I feel relieved that I'm not going. Later I hear that the girls in the upper school, both the French-speaking and the English-speaking ones, found out about the contest, except for Susan, who is not told, as she is assumed to be too young.

SEPTEMBER 3, 1960

In the upper school, everyone knows that Alex and Steve have won the honors for America easily. WaWa, Alex and Steve.

This is also a momentous day for me, as my first experience of going to class with girls begins. Of course, nothing works the way you think it's going to. I think you get to pick the girls and not vice versa. But Susan, the blonde eleven-year old, takes a seat where she can keep her eyes on me. I hope it is a passing interest, as Susan is too young for romance. But as the days turn to weeks, Susan takes to following me around, first at a distance, then next to me, telling me how nice I seem and asking if I will be her boyfriend. I try to ignore her; I tell her I think she is too young to worry about such matters, but she insists everyone else in the upper school does and that she is in love with me. Steve and Alex tease me continuously about this, but I think it is just puppy love and will pass. But that's not what complicated matters.

Karen takes to sitting next to me in class. Steve and Alex tell me they have turned her down as jailbait when she approached them 'to do it." Steve and Alex have long discussions with me about girls and doing it and what to do and what they like. But it is hard to tell whether what they tell me is to impress me or what they tell me is true. Karen sits at an angle so Susan cannot see what she is doing, and she begins to rub the inside of my legs. "Hey!" I whisper. "What's this?"

"Don't you want to do it?" she whispers back.

"OK," I say, "but what about Susan? She follows me everywhere I go. Sometimes she also waits outside the bathroom for me."

"Well," says Karen, "she is an early sleeper in the dorm, and I will wait for you at the window over and down the roof. When you see me, slide over, and I will pull you in. The others may have turned me down, but you better not, unless you want everyone to know that you chickened out on this with me."

I say with my voice thickening, "OK, but if I do, promise me that it will be our secret, and you will wait until the others are behind closed doors."

"Don't worry, this will be fun," Karen says, and moving back to her side of the seat.

I see Susan watching me. After class, Susan comes up to me and asks me what Karen wanted. "Nothing," I mumble hollowly. "She just wanted to know some answers to some questions."

Susan replies, "Well, I don't know everything, but the others say that she is a frustrated bad girl, though I am not sure what that means. I just know if you hang around with her, it's going to ruin things for me. Besides, I'll tell everyone you made me into a bad girl, whatever that means, and nobody will be your girlfriend, even if you think I am too young."

SEPTEMBER 5, 1960

So, I catch Karen in a spare moment, when Susan is being tutored in French, and I tell her what has happened. She says, "Don't worry about what happens if you don't, because I'll add Susan's story to the list of your deeds, and for sure they will call you a cradle-snatcher, if not kick you out of school. As I am two years older than you, what can they say? And Susan's not going to find out. Besides, if she does, my word on the topic is more likely to be believed. Just trust me. I know what I am doing, and she is, as they say, an 'innocent.'"

All day long, my anxiety rises as evening and, then night approaches. That night, I ask Alex about jailbait. He tells me that the girl is underage to do it. I ask what happens if you do and you get caught. He laughs and says, "Then they send you to jail for a long time."

I go down to the room, which I now have for to myself, and try to sleep. The room is small, but has a windowsill that is two inches above the concrete of the building, through which I can see the snow-capped mountains across Lake Geneva. Many times in the art class with Jean LaPierre, the teacher, I enjoyed drawing and thinking about these particular mountains.

I toss and turn and, then go back down to Alex's room and ask, "Well, what if she is older than I am?"

"Well, nothing happens; probably, they just kick you out of school, if they catch you." I was going about to ask him something more, but he interrupts me and says, "Have you something going on? Susan will be jailbait, so don't try that."

So I make up a white lie and say that Nancy has dared me to visit her in the girls' dorms. "Ok," says Alex. "I will watch the window on our side of the dorms, just don't slide off the roof completely, the way that other fellow did and broke his legs. It's 10:00 o'clock. Let's see if anyone is waiting for you in the window of the girls' dorm."

So we go to the window, and sure enough, somebody is waiting. "Well, hero," he says, "put your feet together and your right arm up to catch the ledge and your left arm to keep from going too fast."

Next thing I know, I am sliding down the roof and scrambling for the window. Karen grabs me and pulls me in. "Where have you been? I have been waiting for a while. Let's go to my room," she whispers. She takes my hand and leads me down the corridor, past closed doors, around a corner. "Well," Karen says, "you know what we are here for., Take off your clothes."

It is a bit of a shock to start this way. I have thought it would be more romantic, but I am too numb not to. When it is over, she gives me back my clothes, and whispers in my ear, "I am leaving next week for the States. So Susan can have you back, and we can pretend this never happened."

I nod in the dark, feeling matters have changed from one of those affairs you read about to something I didn't expect. Soon enough, I am crawling back up the roof and Alex is pulling me in through the window.

SEPTEMBER 6, 1960

Everything is as it was before, as though nothing happened. Since Alex cannot see exactly who is at the window, I keep it that way, since it seems safer.

The experience with Karen surprised me; it is a half-step toward the adult experiences I wanted. But it is a half-step backwards in that I have worried too much about what others say and I have nearly hurt Susan. Life and becoming an adult is more complicated than I had imagined. But this is much like WaWa, for who can anticipate it without laughing at my own foolishness?

About the time Karen leaves, my relatives, the Foleys, come to visit me in their VW bus. I do not remember them that well, except for one of the daughters, with whom I have played doctor and nurse in my great -aunt's house in the upper floors, when we are supposed to be taking a nap. My cousin had been chewing bubble -gum, and it had gotten stuck on the pillow and in her braided hair. Tears had fallen down her face, as her mother had to cut the bubble -gum out of her hair. They seem normal and nice to me. In later years, nobody on my father's side discussed them. I think that it is because they live so far away, in Berkeley, California. Actually, in later years, I find out my father's family, the Averills and the Coughlans, have regarded them with suspicion, because they are left-wingers (Socialists) and Dad's family do not want to discuss them in front of the younger generations.

NOVEMBER 15, 1960

In November, the snow begins to stick to the mountain and to the ski slopes above Villars. Soon it is forming a good base, but as that occurs, something happens. Our English-speaking class begins to resist Monsieur James Toby Crighton, or "Tobb the robe," as the students know him. He is a nice teacher, too nice; when the students do not want to do their homework, he lets it be. Of course, Steve and Alex do not do any work from the beginning. Unfortunately—, and I say this in hindsight, —the class resists Monsieur Crighton's teaching us German, so we only learn French, and that too sporadically.

Rumor has it Monsieur Crighton had been a Communist in England and got into some unnamed trouble, either with the Party or the authorities. So here he is coping with a new handful of trouble. I'm not sure what a Communist looks like. He seems a little skinny. Alex and Steve say he is too wimpy. But since we focus on French two classes a day, it feels like one day I do not understand French and the next day I can think in a basic fashion in French. The accent is the key. It is like an attitude and is graded into Parisian French, which is the best, plus ordinary French, that the shopkeepers speak, plus the Vadouis peasant French. So we learn all the different accents and ways to speak French, for fun. WaWa.

NOVEMBER 20, 1960

Monsieur Boulangé is the headmaster, and he always addresses us in French. That's how I find out about poor Alain. He has messed up the urinals, as he can not wait. Monsieur Boulangé is furious, and he makes the entire school stand at attention for an hour and a half, until someone confesses. The second time this happens, I am there. Alain is asked to stay behind. This time, he has clogged up the toilet with such a big movement that it will not flush. All the boys have to go and look, of course. Poor Alain, how embarrassing it must have been! WaWa.

DECEMBER 20, 1960- –JANUARY 1, 1960-61

Skiing and skating season has arrived. Monsieur Rudy Rennard teaches me the basics of skiing. I fall all over the mountain at first, but being young and enthusiastic, I learn to Stem Christie (this means being able to move the skis in a "V" while bobbing up and down) and then Christie by shifting my weight from one ski to another. It is intoxicating! I go as fast as I dare. As Christmas vacation comes, Dad and Mom say they cannot come till spring. I have to stay at Villars. However, Dad says he has a Christmas present for me that I will appreciate.

It is ski lessons. My expert instructor takes me to the top of the best trails, and I ski down. Then I watch him. Next, he gives me some pointers in French. Then he does the rest of the trails with me hot on his heels. After a few hours, I am on my own. The skiing cuts the loneliness of not going home to Africa. Of course, I miss WaWa, but I think I will make a ski team in the States. WaWa Swiss skiing. Every day the mountain has a covering of light, powdered snow. I will be first up the train to the T-bar and the gondolas to the top of the mountain for the big runs. Only the trails of the ski patrols will precede me. It is perfect snow conditions, with clear, sunny days followed by more snow at night. After a while, school resumes, so school takes up my mornings, but afternoons are free for skiing.

MARCH 15, 1961

In the spring, the snow turns to "corn snow" (corn snow is snow that's like corn in the sense that it's crunchy and it's produced in the cold of the night and warm spring days), and my parents finally arrive. It is good to see them, as I am a bit homesick by then. When they arrive, I go over to their hotel. They ask me to order breakfast, to show off my French. So in Parisian French I ask, "Does anybody speak English down there?" There is somebody who does, so I order three continental breakfasts for my parents and Coagie. My parents are very amused by my tactics.

They ask me to invite my friends for dinner, so I ask Steve and Alex to come with their girlfriends. Steve's girlfriend does not come, but Alex's girlfriend comes, along with her sister, who turns out to be Susan. Susan sits and stares at me all night. My parents think she is very nice. I am embarrassed at the obvious nature of her affection. We order cheese fondue and meat fondue. The trick of eating fondue is to cook the meat well enough before dipping it in the melted cheese. As usual, I burn my mouth, and that reduces my conversation to mumbling. Steve and Alex develop all sorts of manners and the politest language I have ever heard them use. Since I have written a lot to my parents about Steve and Alex, after dinner Dad and Mom say I must have been exaggerating about them, since they seem like such nice boys. What can I say?

My parents stay long enough for my mother to go ice-skating. She tries some skiing but shakes the T-bar because her leg is bothering her. Later in the States, the doctor says she had had a polio attack in Africa.

My father rents skis and follows me down the mountain, skiing next to the train as I race ahead, stopping for my father to catch up and then racing ahead again. All too quickly, my parents and Coagie are gone.

We plan a final ski trip; it is planned for up in the German section of Switzerland, since the snow has melted at Villars. It is a resort near Zurich, I believe. What makes an impression on me is the fact that the T- bar is still buried up to the top of the t bar pole except where the snow had been cut away. Skiing is in spring corn snow, but the resort is so high up in the mountain that the air is thinner,. So one does not do as many runs without feeling it. My parents tell me I will be returning to prep school that summer and I will be staying with my aunt until school starts.

LATE APRIL, 1961

Late spring is great. In the afternoons, we play a giant version of capture the flag on the mountain and the valleys, behind Villars. Every Swiss cow has its own sounding bell and its own name. WaWa, Swiss cows. The upper pastures are larger, so we will run up and down them, hiding between remnants of haystacks and the small farm buildings. The farmers do not mind, as long as we leave the cows alone. They can tell from the sounds of the bells approximately where the cows are. There are even goats around with bells like the cows, but they are smaller, not only the goats but also the bells. WaWa.

As spring turns to summer, I wonder why some of the boys get to go on the glacier climbs and I have to go on the long walks with the others. Later I find out, my parents have put a stop to glacier climbs, for fear something might happen. WaWa, parents.

JULY 1961

Switzerland, like West Africa, has its own WaWa's. For example, each faction-- —Swiss French, Swiss Italian, Swiss-Swiss, and Swiss German, is like a tribal society. Each has its own sense of itself. As I remember it, the WaWa's are based on food and culture. But most of all, food. The Swiss French are into hot goat's milk in the afternoons, which I think tastes terrible. The Swiss Italians are represented by spaghetti and meatballs, which is a great WaWa treat. The Swiss -Swiss are into cheese with holes in it, milk chocolate, and my all- time favorite, white chocolate, which is so sweet, it makes your teeth ache for more. WaWa. Of course, there is also Swiss fondue, which divides into cheese fondue, which I imagine is invented by the Swiss French, who love all sorts of cheese, including some that smells bad but still manages to taste good. And last but not least, the Swiss Germans are into meat fondue. The main problem and challenge is not to burn your mouth while popping fire-hot morsels into it. WaWa. Soon enough, it is the end of my school year in Switzerland. The police find my passport and turn it in to the school. It is a blessing and a relief. This time, I am staying with my Aunt Sally before going to boarding school in the United States. A new chapter of my life is to begin, but that is a story for another time. One more time I say WaWa and wish you fine, fine pass Takoradi self.

INDEX

A

Accra 3, 4, 10, 15, 20, 23, 25, 26,
  29, 42, 43, 49, 76, 87, 92, 94,
  98, 102, 105, 106, 114
alleluvia 37
Allez, Allez 127
Assumaja-Hene 36, 37
Azores 3

B

Boeuf Bourguignon 8
Bon Noveau élève suivez moi 126
bush 2, 10, 12, 21, 27, 44, 48, 50,
  78, 79, 92, 93, 95, 98, 100

C

conkers 71, 72
croquet set 6

D

diker 13, 14, 118
Dis be good t'ing 18

E

éclairs 8
elephantiastis 21

F

fine-fine past Takoradi self 113
fla-fla boy 21, 24, 80
fou fou 14

G

gari 14
Guz 71

H

Hausa people 22, 107, 117
Humber Hawk 36

J

Ju-ju viii, 11, 12, 15, 21, 22, 23,
  30, 32, 49, 65

L

Laufia lo 11

M

mammy wagon 10, 31, 32, 101
millipede 7
Moshie Greyhound 27

O

on ya somi, on ya toto, on ya gormi
  18, 19

P

pickens 7, 42, 96
pink gins 19
plantain 10, 96
Plava House 12, 22, 23, 24
Portuguese man-o-war 86, 87

R

red scorpions 99
rents 16, 17, 24, 25, 51, 54, 64, 75,
  80, 88, 114, 117, 120, 138

S

some dash 106
Stratocruiser 2

T

Takoradi 20, 44, 113, 139
tuppence 36
two-shilling 8, 9, 87

V

very dear 95

W

wallflower 129
WaWa i, ii, iii, v, vii, viii, 1, 8,
11, 12, 13, 14, 15, 16, 17, 19,
21, 25, 26, 27, 29, 30, 32, 38,
39, 41, 43, 46, 48, 49, 50, 53,
54, 56, 57, 58, 59, 60, 63, 64,
65, 66, 69, 73, 74, 76, 78, 79,
80, 81, 82, 84, 85, 88, 91, 93,
96, 97, 99, 100, 101, 102, 103,
104, 105, 109, 110, 112, 113,
114, 116, 118, 119, 120, 123,
125, 127, 129, 131, 135, 136,
137, 138, 139

Y

Yacetti 89, 90
Yacettio 89
You dey be sorry soon 18